OZ
Graphix
[5]

A showcase of work from top Australian design studios

Graphic design
Illustration
Photography

CONTENTS

The studios

Introduction	9
Foreword	11
Afterimage Graphic Design and Photography	14
AG Design	15
APR Design	16
Balance Design Group	18
Bastian Group	20
Black Squid Design	17
Blue Marlin Brand Design	22
Brave Communications	26
Cowan Design	28
David Trewern Design (DTDesign)	30
DeMo Design	32
designCentric	34
Design Itch	38
Disegno Group	36
Emma Broe	39
Genie Creative	40
Girling Design	41
house mouse design	42
HSJ Design Group	43
Icon Partners	44
Icon Raremedia	46
Ident	48
Image & Substance	50
Interbrand Australia	52
ism Graphic Design	54
Joseph Casni Design Management	56
Latitude Group	58
Liveworm Studio	60
Mekanica	61
MDM Design Associates	62
Monitor Graphics	66
Moon Design	64
Percept Creative Group	67
PhD	68
Plutonium	70
Rokat Design	72
RP Brown	74
Show & Tell Creative	76
Simon Bowden Design (SB+D)	75
Sprout Creative	78
Storm Creative	83
Studio218	82
Studio Equator	80
The Graphic Image Studio	84
Tracey Allen	85
Triple 888 Studios	86
Underline: Fitch	88
Visible Ink Design	87

Illustrators

Bill Wood	94
D MAX	96
Deborah Niland	97
Dee Texidor - Illustrator and Designer	98
Double Happy	99
Ian F Faulkner & Associates	102
James Hart Design	100
Medical Arts - Dr Levent EFE, CMI	104
The Mutation Parlour - Jason Atherton	103
NZ Illustration	105
Squidinc Illustration and Design	106
Susy Boyer	107

Photographers

Australian Scenics	110
Maynard Imaging	111
Momentum Studio	112
sam i am photo	114

Associations	118
Order form	123
Company index	126
Sponsors	137

CONTENTS BY STATE

ACT	Studio218	82
NSW	AG Design	15
	Balance Design Group	18
	Blue Marlin Brand Design	22
	Brave Communications	26
	Cowan Design	28
	David Trewern Design (DTDesign)	30
	Deborah Niland	97
	Dee Texidor - Illustrator and Designer	98
	DeMo Design	32
	Design Itch	38
	Genie Creative	40
	Ian F Faulkner & Associates	102
	Ident	48
	Joseph Casni Design Management	56
	MDM Design Associates	62
	Moon Design	64
	The Mutation Parlour - Jason Atherton	103
	Percept Creative Group	67
	PhD	68
	RP Brown	74
	sam i am photo	114
	Storm Creative	83
	Triple 888 Studios	86
	Underline: Fitch	88
NT	Sprout Creative	78
QLD	Liveworm Studio	60
	Maynard Imaging	111
	Momentum Studio	112
	Susy Boyer	107
SA	Black Squid Design	17
	designCentric	34
	Image & Substance	50
	NZ Illustration	105

TAS	Tracey Allen	85
VIC	Afterimage Graphic Design and Photography	14
	APR Design	16
	Australian Scenics	110
	Bastian Group	20
	Bill Wood	94
	Blue Marlin Brand Design	22
	Cowan Design	28
	D MAX	96
	David Trewern Design (DTDesign)	30
	Disegno Group	36
	Double Happy	99
	Girling Design	41
	house mouse design	42
	HSJ Design Group	43
	Icon Partners	44
	Icon Raremedia	46
	Interbrand Australia	52
	ism Graphic Design	54
	James Hart Design	100
	Latitude Group	58
	MDM Design Associates	62
	Medical Arts - Dr Levent EFE, CMI	104
	Mekanica	61
	Monitor Graphics	66
	Plutonium	70
	Rokat Design	72
	Show & Tell Creative	76
	Simon Bowden Design (SB+D)	75
	Squidinc Illustration and Design	106
	Studio Equator	80
	The Graphic Image Studio	84
	Visible Ink Design	87
WA	Emma Broe	39

INTRODUCTION

Feast your eyes on the work of some of Australia's top design studios in this, the fifth edition of Oz Graphix. As the pace of life has increased, so has our dependence on visual cues and graphic imagery. As a general rule, people nowadays lead much more intricate lives. The messages come thick and fast and pictures get the main messages across more efficiently every time.

In today's world, the job of the designer is to interpret and prepare concepts, offers, proposals and information. Graphic images delight, inform and entertain us. In Oz Graphix 5, we showcase the work of skillful designers, illustrators and photographers. They reflect our culture and show who we are and who we would like to be.

I am pleased to offer you another serving of top Australian creativity. Enjoy.

Colin Wood
Publisher

Design exists in so much of what we see in our daily lives—from brochures to branding, packaging to photography, corporate identities to illustrations, not to mention logos and websites.

Now in its fifth edition, Oz Graphix once again showcases the quality and magnitude of work produced by top Australian graphic designers, illustrators and photographers. Those featured in this publication contribute in today's world market and, with their creative abilities, show Australian design to be world class.

I'm pleased to be able to present this showcase of inspiring work and I hope you enjoy Oz Graphix [5] as much as I enjoyed bringing it to you.

Loueze Harper
Project Editor

FOREWORD

As an important part of our role in the Australian graphic design industry, AGDA (Australian Graphic Design Association) is delighted to continue its association with Oz Graphix.

A key part of what we need to do as visual communicators is provide our audiences with the appropriate reference points which help define our contribution to business and the arts in a cultural, social and economic context. By showcasing our talents, Oz Graphix not only provides such an environment, it also serves as an important reference point for business, our industry and for our students.

On behalf of AGDA I would like to congratulate all those whose work is contained within these pages.

I would also like to congratulate the publishers. There is no doubt whatsoever that the best Australian design is at least the equal of the best from around the world. Oz Graphix is now a well established forum for Australian design and as such is a very significant national and international ambassador.

Design is a language that builds relationships... and relationships generally work best when they share information, inspiration and pleasure. Oz Graphics achieves all three.

Enjoy it.

Simon Pemberton
AGDA National President

agda.com.au

Oz Graphix [5]

THE STUDIOS

Afterimage Graphic Design and Photography

21 Budd Street
Collingwood VIC 3066

Phone: 03 9416 3689
Fax: 03 9416 2998

www.afterimage.com.au
admin@afterimage.com.au

Afterimage pride themselves on their mutually beneficial partnership with clients, offering a wealth of information and support in design, advertising, marketing and related areas. Established in 1990, Afterimage values its reputation in producing exceptional work across a range of industries. The talented and innovative team possess a wide variety of skills and expertise in design and advertising. They provide a complete service from concept to implementation and delivery for catalogues, brochures, advertising, corporate identity, digital photography and web design. Afterimage reflects the true nature of their clients' business by developing an in-depth understanding of their products and services. They offer personalised attention, including ongoing consultation and follow-up at every stage of production.

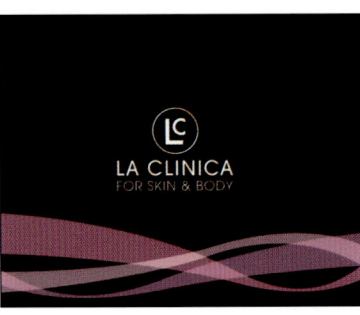
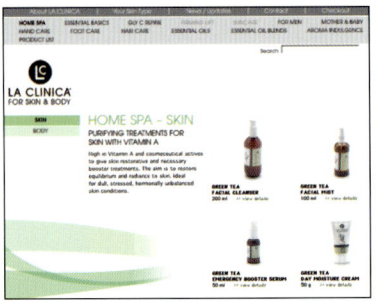

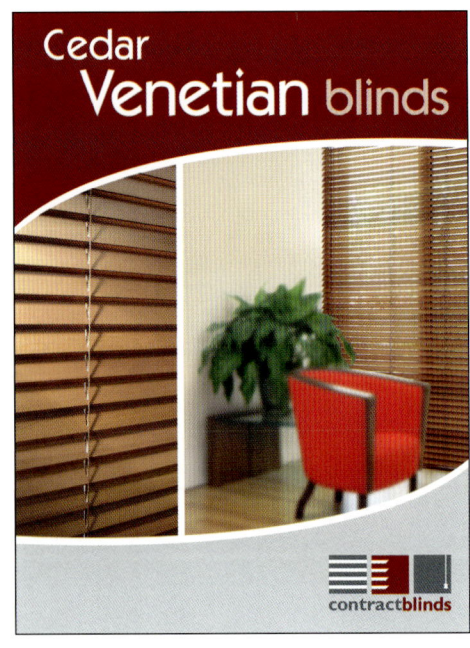

(top left)
Project Family health care product packaging
Client Parker Healthcare

(top centre)
Project Website
Client La Clinica

(top right)
Project Logos
Client Seldex Artisticalbums
Client Contract Blinds
Client Delf Architectural Hardware

(above left)
Project Product catalogue
Client Cornall (Merchandise)

(above centre)
Project Product catalogue
Client Woods Furniture

(above right)
Project Product leaflets
Client Contract Blinds

Anna Godwin, Sydney based designer and illustrator, creates mostly digital imagery for the publishing, advertising and design industries. A background in design enables her to understand and take a productive role in the creative process, producing pencil roughs and visualising ideas at concept stage. Although her style lends itself to children's illustration and character development, Anna receives a wide variety of commissions from clients locally and overseas.

AG Design

Mobile: 0405 432 866

www.agdesign.net.au
anna@agdesign.net.au

(top left)
Project 'Kid'
Medium Digital
Client Artist's portfolio

(top right)
Project 'Mervin' the Monkey
Medium Digital
Client Sara Lee - school canteen muffins packaging

(above left)
Project Penguin
Medium Digital
Client Aldi - White Flakes cereal packaging

(above right)
Project 'The Race'
Medium Digital
Client Artist's portfolio

APR Design

96-98 Bluff Road
Black Rock VIC 3193

Phone: 03 9598 3588
Fax: 03 9597 0630

www.aprdesign.com.au
info@aprdesign.com.au

APR Design are design specialists providing packaging solutions and below-the-line advertising support to high profile FMCG companies. Our dedicated team works closely with marketing and sales professionals to build a solid strategic approach, coupled with exceptional creative to ensure success for every project.

(top left)
Project M&M's 3D Easter character
Client Masterfoods Australia/NZ

(top right)
Project Dig Tree wine labels
Client Burke & Wills Winery

(centre)
Project SPC Ardmona Food Service support material
Client SPC Ardmona

(above)
Project Goulburn Valley Fruit Snacks
Client SPC Ardmona

Design based around ideas generation and visual communication, to do the unexpected, accept risk and emphasise what is new, maintaining identity and appeal. Design intellectually driven solutions that best answer the clients' brief. To explore all avenues remembering the element of surprise. But most importantly – have fun.

Black Squid Design

203 Melbourne Street
North Adelaide SA 5006

Phone: 08 8361 8066

www.blacksquid.com.au
info@blacksquid.com.au

(top)
Project Wine labels
Client Griffin Wines

(above left to right)
Project Corporate identity for marketing company
Client hamrahead

Project Corporate identity for homewares store
Client Uccello

Project Handle with care flyers
Client Swanport Harvest Staycrisp Lettuce

Project Corporate identity for computer systems company
Client Big Fish Systems

Oz Graphix [5]   17

Balance Design Group

PO Box 1425
Neutral Bay NSW 2089

Phone: 02 9922 1099
Fax: 02 8920 1768

www.balance.com.au
stuart@balance.com.au

We were born to design! **Balance Design Group** is a Sydney based agency specialising in corporate branding, dynamic website design and systems development. With over twenty years in business, and nine years digital experience, behind us, clients can be assured of high quality creative combined with smooth project implementation. Our experience and history has made Balance Design one of the most effective and well respected digital agencies in Sydney.

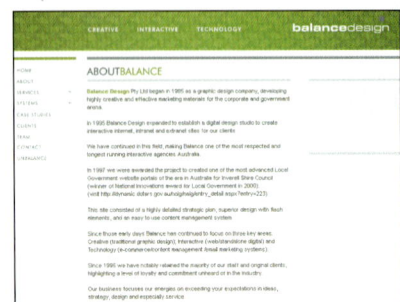

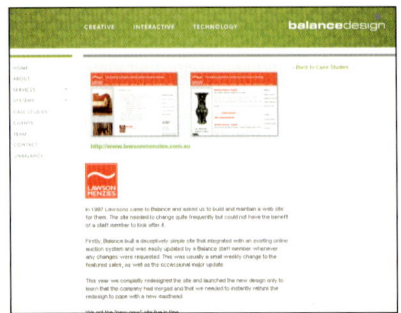

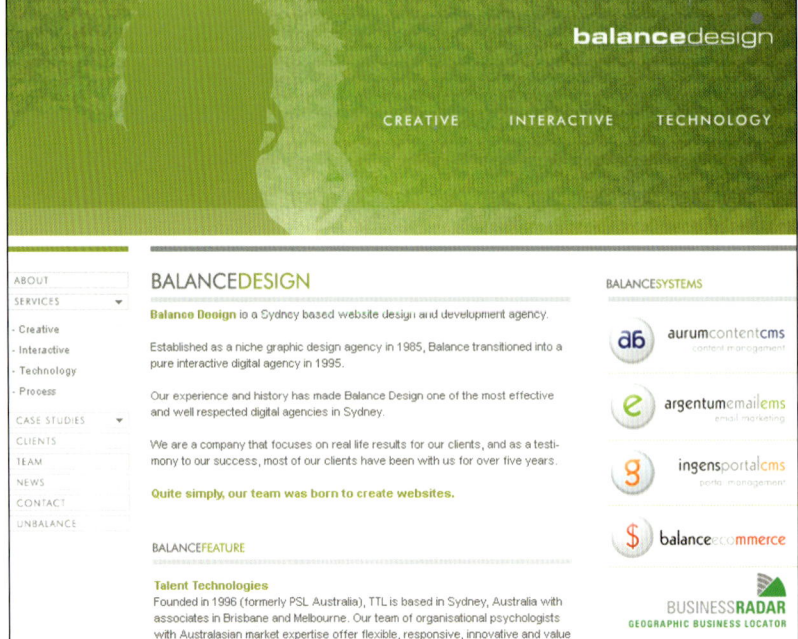

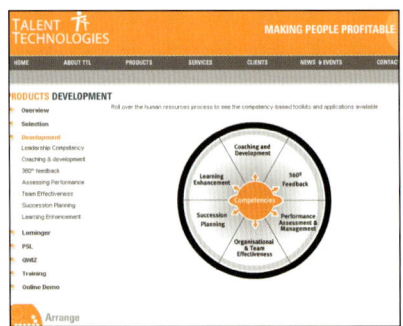

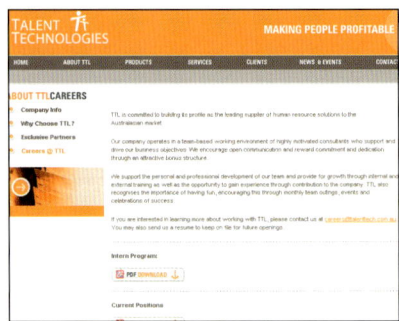

(top, series)
Project Website design & development
Client Balance Design
www.balance.com.au
Creative Director Shane Allen

(above, series)
Project IT
Client Talent Technologies
www.talenttechnologies.com.au
Creative Director Shane Allen

18   Oz Graphix [5]

Balance Design Group

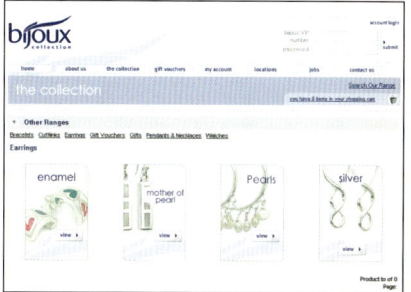
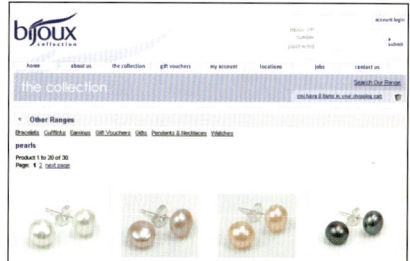

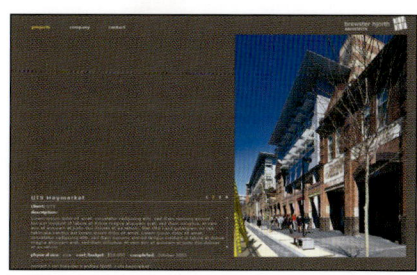

(top, series)
Project Jewellery
Client Bijoux Collection
www.bijoux.com.au

(above, series)
Project Architecture
Client Brewster Hjorth Architects
www.brewsterhjorth.com.au

Oz Graphix [5]   19

Phone: 03 8676 7504
Fax: 03 8676 7505

www.bastiangroup.com.au
info@bastiangroup.com.au

no illusions that the challenge is to find smarter ways of developing new communication models and practices that will advance our clients' competitive market positioning. This we believe can

marketing and branding to design, packaging and corporate identity services. Our range of services are centralised around our strategic way of thinking—we are not afraid to ask the question, why?

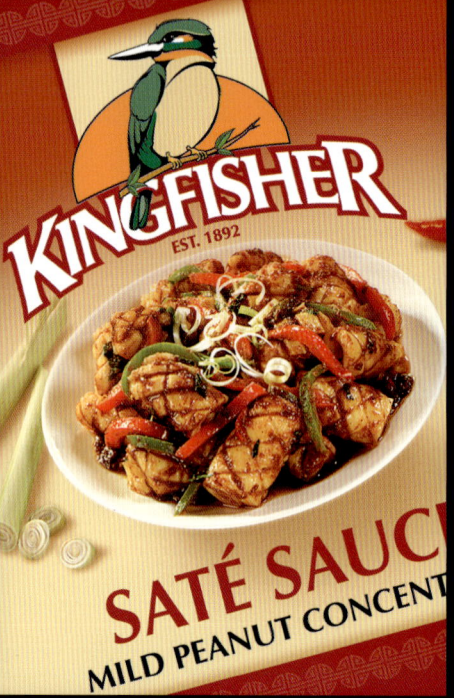

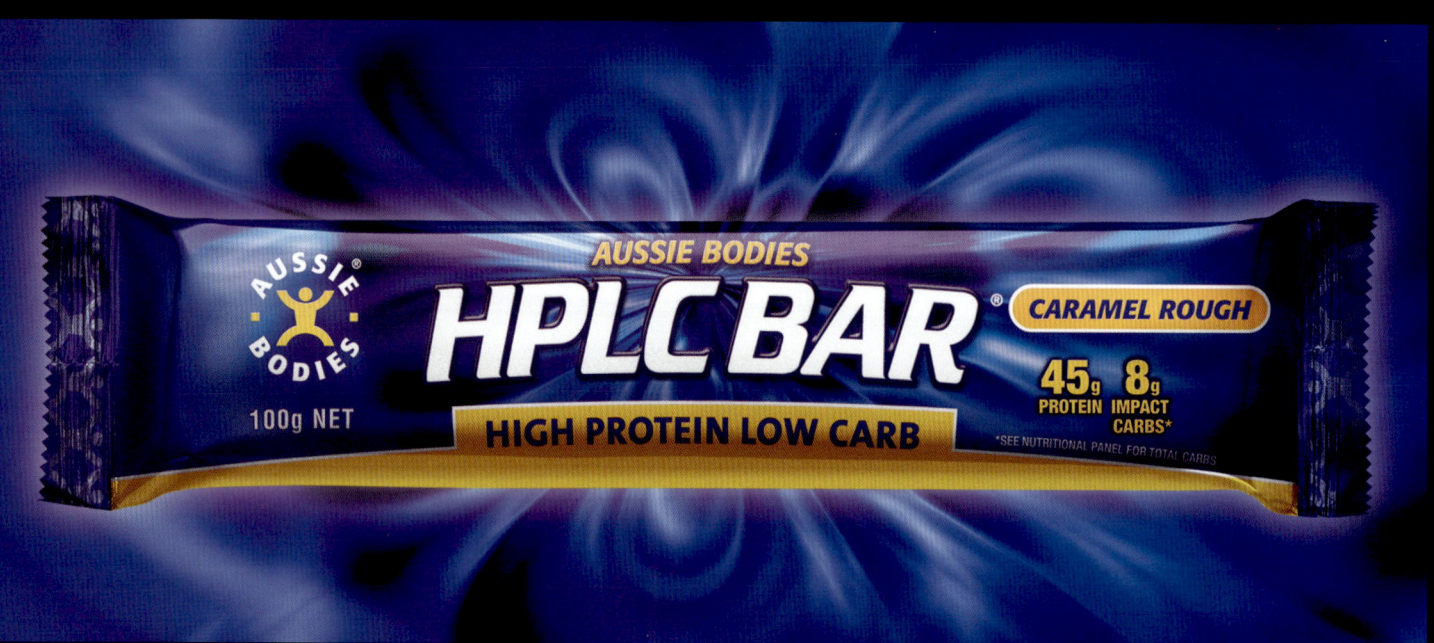

(top left)
Project Branding & packaging launch for FMCG (national & international)
Client Lee Seng Heng (Hong Kong)

(top centre)
Project Aloe drink brand redesign
Client Koya Korea

(top right)
Project Berconia Coffee brand identity & packaging
Client Berconia (Hong Kong)

(above)
Project HPLC Bar brand redesign
Client Aussie Bodies

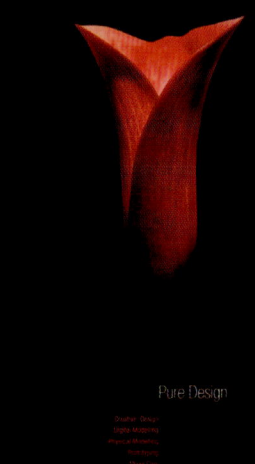

(top left)
Project Midsumma campaign (poster, guide & promotional collateral)
Client Midsumma Melbourne

(top right)
Project St Kilda Festival Campaign 2005 (poster, guide & promotional collateral)
Client City of Port Phillip

(above left)
Project Alaqua campaign
Client Koya Korea

(above centre)
Project Triple R Radiothon campaign
Client Triple R Broadcasters

(above right)
Project Pure Design campaign
Client Technicon Australia

Blue Marlin Brand Design

Melbourne
7 Meaden Street
Southbank VIC 3006

Sydney
Level 3, 5 Queen Street
Chippendale NSW 2008

Phone: 03 9694 5900
Fax: 03 9694 5999

Phone: 02 9698 3277
Fax: 02 9698 2677

www.bluemarlinbd.com
ozcrew1@bluemarlinbd.com.au

Blue Marlin is a strategically focused brand design agency that delivers outstanding identity, graphic and structural packaging design for many of Australia's key FMCG and retail companies.
By focusing on complete consumer & brand environment understanding, we produce creative solutions that achieve considerable cut-through for our clients' brands. This approach is applied to visual and corporate identity as well as product innovation, NPD and in-depth brand strategy. Highlighted here is a snapshot of our Australian work, all of which achieved or exceeded our clients' marketing objectives through comprehensive and effective brand design solutions. While we continuously focus on each market's independent nuances, our global resources in Australia, the

(left)
Project New brand design - Aquaveta
Client Cadbury Schweppes

(centre)
Project New range design - Kettle Crunch Cut
Client Arnott's Snackfoods

(right)
Project Brand redesign - Sorbent
Client SCA Hygiene Australasia

(left)
Project Brand redesign - Always Fresh
Client Riviana Foods

(centre)
Project Brand design - Lifestyles
Client Ansell Healthcare

(right)
Project Brand design - Friskies
Client Nestlé Purina

Brave Communications

Level 3, 55 Chandos Street
St Leonards NSW 2065

Phone: 02 9439 2344
Fax: 02 9439 4537

www.bravecomm.com.au
studio@bravecomm.com.au

Brave Communications is a strategic design consultancy offering a comprehensive range of services; brand strategy, packaging (graphics & form), corporate communications and brand activation—thus delivering an integrated experience across all areas of visual communication.
We believe that strong brands are built on a shared vision of the future; on true customer and market understanding.

Together with our clients, we create solutions that are brave, dynamic and innovative.
In a Brave future, the businesses that will grow and make a difference are those that embrace change, and are willing to acquire the new skills and capabilities needed to do so.

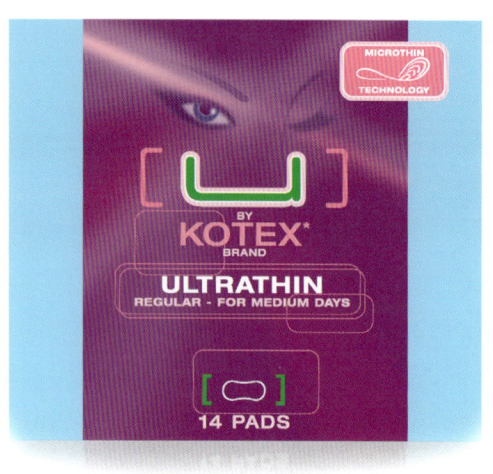

(top)
Project 'Tonight' range of sauces
Client Unilever Continental

(above left)
Project 'U' by Kotex range
Client Kimberly-Clark

(above, series)
Project Streets packaging and brand activation
Client Unilever Streets

Brave Communications

(above)
Project 'Mt Franklin' form design and rebranding
Client Coca-Cola Australia

(above right)
Project 'CC's' rebranding
Client Arnott's

(bottom right)
Project 'Sizzle & Stir' packaging
Client Unilever Continental

Cowan

Melbourne
220 High Street
Prahran VIC 3181

Sydney
239 Pacific Highway
North Sydney NSW 2060

Phone: 03 9521 2422
Fax: 03 9521 2929

Phone: 02 9929 9177
Fax: 02 9929 3672

www.cowandesign.com

Creating
At Cowan, we understand the importance of achieving a balance between the emotional and rational cues within brand campaigns. Such balance is crucial if brand values and product benefits are to be communicated successfully. Through creativity, essential information can be delivered in a memorable way to demand the desired response from the target audience.

(left)
Project Cap'n BirdsEye
Client Simplot

(centre)
Project Tub range
Client Sara Lee

(right)
Project Salada
Client Arnott's

28 Oz Graphix [5]

Brand
A brand is more than a logo.
It is a powerful visual language that communicates with the consumer and creates a lasting bond. Fundamental to our philosophy is the understanding of the relationship that can be developed between the brand and the consumer.
Our process forges links and delivers clear messages to the market, without relying on words alone.

Campaigns
The prosperity of a brand is not dependent on any individual piece of communication, but a multifaceted program of events delivered over time. In any brand project, our design strategies are based upon the bigger picture. This provides a platform for campaigns that are carefully constructed, specifically targeted and cleverly executed.

Cowan

(left)
Project Asian Soups
Client Heinz

(centre)
Project Drumstick Loaded
Client Nestlé Peters

(right)
Project Yoplait
Client National Foods

David Trewern Design (DTDesign)

Melbourne
117 Green Street
Richmond VIC 3121

Phone: 03 9429 2799
Fax: 03 9429 8706

www.dtdesign.com
info@dtdesign.com

Sydney (STW Group)
Level 45, Citigroup Centre
2 Park Street
Sydney NSW 2000

Phone: 02 9268 1735

David Trewern Design (DTDesign) is a specialist internet development studio, focusing on creatively-driven internet strategy, design and technology. Founded in 1996, it is one of Australia's most innovative, experienced and awarded web development firms.

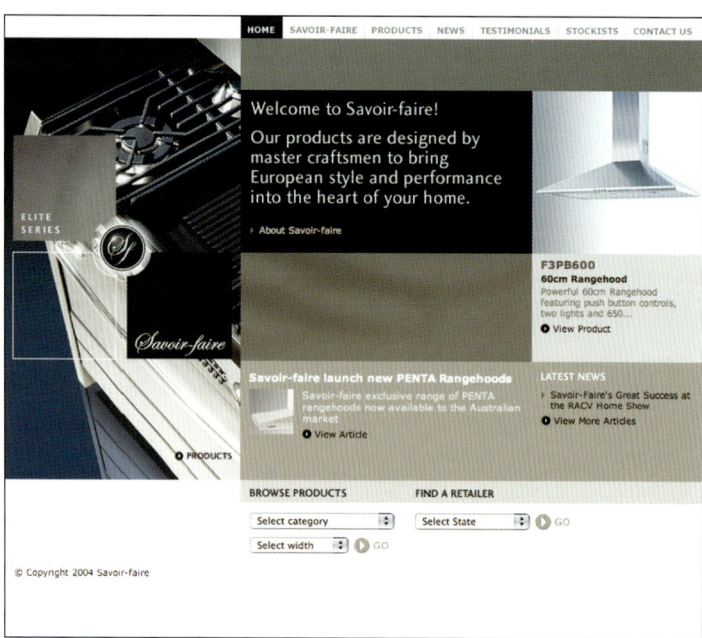

(top left)
Project Tabcorp website
www.tabcorp.com.au
Client Tabcorp Australia

(top right)
Project Savoir-faire website
www.savoir-faire.com.au
Client Savoir-faire

(above left)
Project Adrenalin website
www.adrenalin.com.au
Client Live Adrenalin

(above right)
Project Oxia website
www.oxia.com
Client Oxia

David Trewern Design (DTDesign)

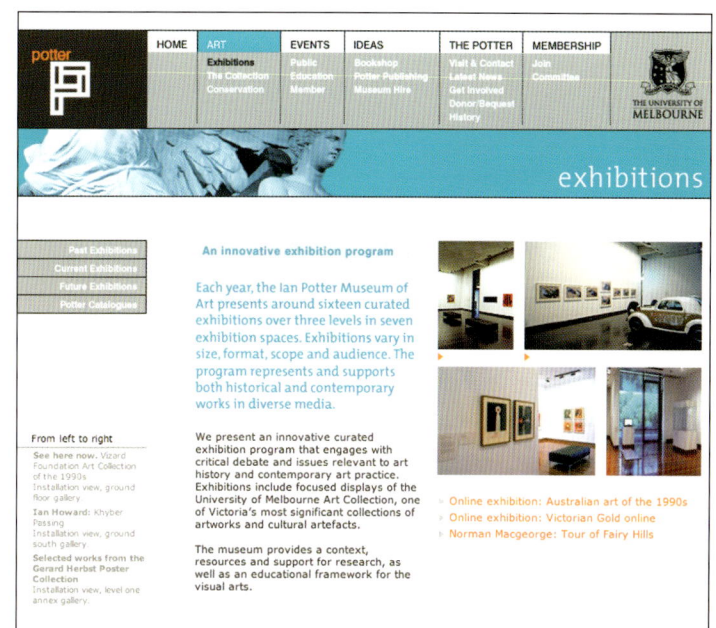
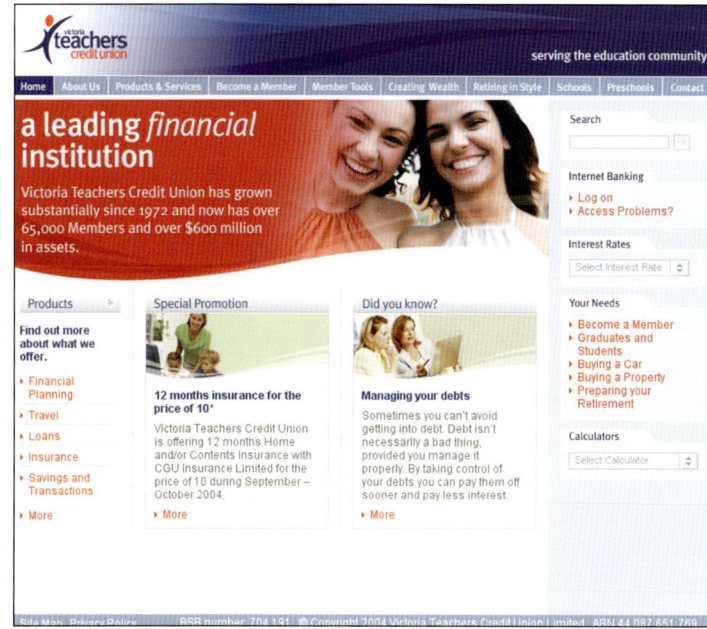
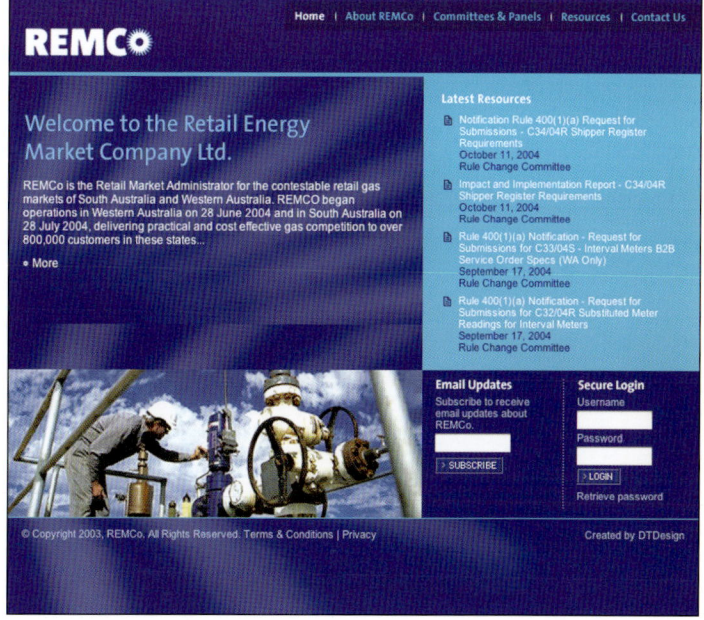

(top left)
Project Provincial Victoria website
www.provincialvictoria.vic.gov.au
Client Victorian Government

(top right)
Project The Ian Potter Museum of Art website
www.art-museum.unimelb.edu.au/
Client The Ian Potter Museum of Art, The University of Melbourne

(above left)
Project Victoria Teachers Credit Union website
www.victeach.com.au
Client Victoria Teachers Credit Union

(above right)
Project REMCo website
www.remco.net.au
Client REMCo

DeMo Design

373 Riley Street
Surry Hills NSW 2010

Phone: 02 9211 2966
Fax: 02 9211 2969

www.demodesign.com.au
mail@demodesign.com.au

DeMo are specialists in packaging design for FMCG.
Our personable, creative team focuses on outstanding and innovative solutions, because innovation lies at the heart of both better design and better business.
Through dialogue with our clients, we bridge the gap between brand strategy and brand execution, communicating core values to make a positive connection with the consumer. Our design expertise includes; new product development, brand updates, structural packaging and research stimulus.

(top left)
Title Kit Kat Mint Rush—new product variant packaging design
Client Nestlé Confectionery

(top right)
Title Butter Menthol—packaging update
Client Nestlé Australasia

(above left)
Title Hokkien Noodles range—new product range packaging design
Client Cypress & Sons Pty Ltd

(above right)
Title Nestlé Bites range—new product range packaging design
Client Nestlé Confectionery

DeMo Design

(top left)
Title Milo Energy Bar—new product variant packaging design
Client Nestlé Confectionery

(top right)
Title Westons Cream Addictions range—new product range packaging design
Client George Westons Foods Ltd

(above left)
Title Gondoliers International Pantry—new product range packaging design
Client Cypress & Sons Pty Ltd

(above right)
Title Nestlé Malted Milk—packaging update
Client Nestlé Foods & Beverages

Designers/Art Directors
Paul Devonshire & Lisa Molloy

designCentric

163 Gilles Street
Adelaide SA 5000

Phone: 08 8232 3377
Fax: 08 8232 3766

www.designcentric.com.au
ask@designcentric.com.au

designCentric continues to be chosen by clients who value innovation, creativity and functionality in design. With an excellent record of project management, designCentric offers the complete range of graphic design, brand development and strategic communications.

(logos, top left to right)
Project Corporate identity and branding
Client UMCOS Trading

Project Corporate identity and branding
Client Dovetail Designs

Project Corporate identity and branding
Client Elysion

(top right)
Project Website redesign
Client Zero Waste SA

(above)
Project Marketing brochure
Client Tonkin Consulting

34 Oz Graphix [5]

designCentric

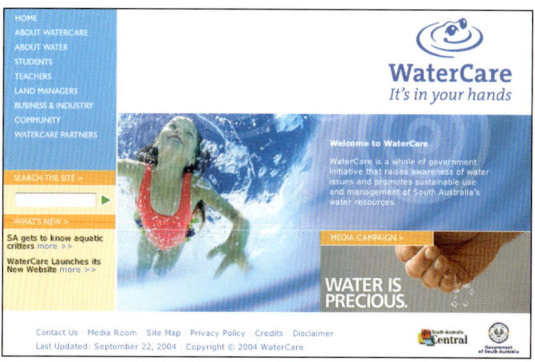

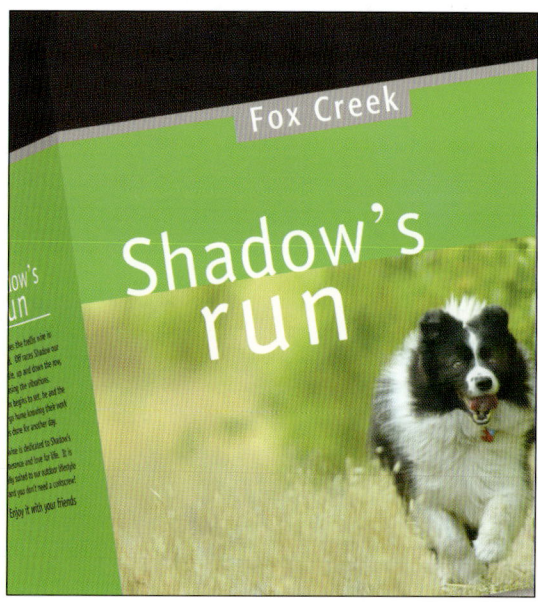

(top left)
Project Conference identity and branding
Client Managed Innovation International

(top right)
Project New product branding website
Client San Remo

(centre right)
Project Website redesign
Client WaterCare

(above left)
Project Function Centre branding and displays
Client SA Water

(above right)
Project Packaging design
Client Fox Creek Winery

Oz Graphix [5] 35

Disegno Group

129 Queensbridge Street
Southbank VIC 3006

Phone: 03 9690 0905
Fax: 03 9690 0906

www.disegno.com.au
enquiry@disegno.com.au

Disegno brings corporate and brand management, strategic marketing and creative visual thinking together to solve clients' marketing challenges. Combining extensive experience in Australia and overseas with a young, committed team, the group can handle projects of all sizes, from corporate design to product packaging to in-house internet project design and implementation.
A loyal clientele and successful track record prove the effectiveness and value of Disegno's integrated approach.

(top left)
Project Perfect Italiano range repackaging
Client Bonland Dairies

(top right)
Project Mainland Spreadable Feta range packaging
Client Bonland Dairies

(above)
Project Original Sunnyboy range repackaging
Client Berri Ltd

Disegno Group

(above)
Project Bogie Man brand development and packaging
Client Watson's Vineyard

Oz Graphix [5] **37**

Design Itch

1a Chapman Street
Charlestown NSW 2290

Phone: 02 4943 6623
Fax: 02 4943 6624

www.designitch.com.au
hello@designitch.com.au

Design Itch is always ready for creative challenges and new itches to scratch.

Since 1999, Design Itch has been creating fresh design solutions to help a variety of organisations achieve their unique goals.

They have eagerly invested much time developing a specialised design process to ensure seamless project management, and they believe that good relationships and open communication form the basis of successful design.

Design Itch insists on creating results-orientated solutions that deliver a positive image of confidence, professionalism and individuality.

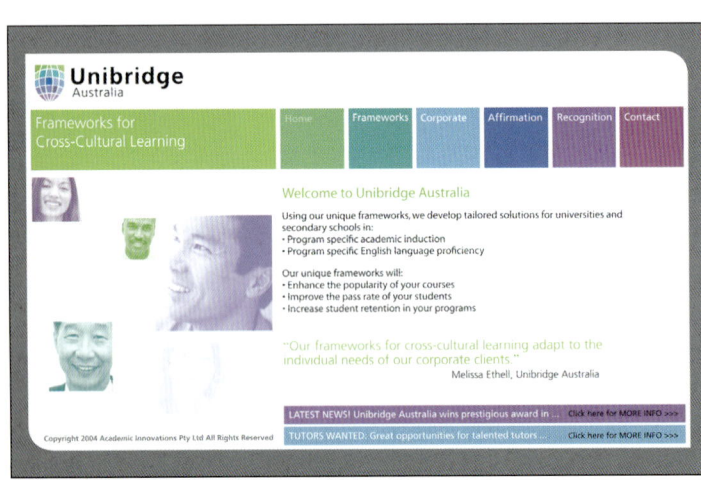

(top left)
Project Corporate sales brochure
Client DELL Financial Services

(centre left)
Project Brand and website
Client Unibridge Australia

(above)
Project DM brochure
Client Morfurniture

(top right)
Project Logo
Client Crysalis Hair Sanctuary & Beauty Boudoir

(centre right)
Project Logo
Client AMSI | Australian Mining Services International

Emma Broe has over 13 years experience in all aspects of graphic design and web development from concepts to application, in areas ranging from packaging, point of sale and corporate literature through to international magazine design and advertising.
Clients include: Ford UK, Nissan GB, Henkel, Department of Education & Training, WA and businesses based both Australia wide and overseas.

Emma Broe

Lot 80, Castle Street
Kirup WA 6251

Phone: 08 9731 6450
Fax: 08 9731 6450

www.emmabroe.com
emmabroe@wn.com.au

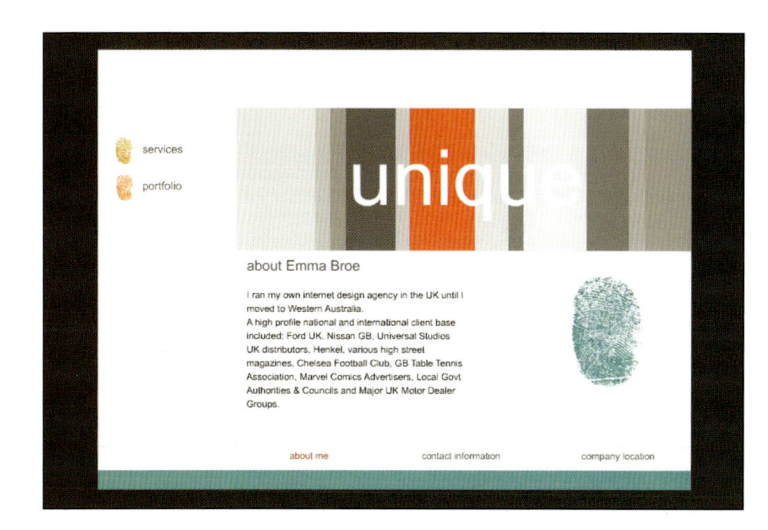

(top left)
Project Website (flash)
Client Self promotion

(top right)
Project Website featuring full product range
Client Sol-Creations

(above)
Project Billboard as part of a marketing campaign series
Client Sol-Creations

Oz Graphix [5]   39

Genie Creative

Level 2, 21 Oxford Street
Darlinghurst NSW 2010

Phone: 02 9283 4700

www.geniecreative.com.au
info@geniecreative.com.au

Genie Creative are specialists in web design and development, flash animation and online advertising. They excel in creating a diverse selection of online solutions that mixes outstanding creativity with intuitive functionality. They have produced work for AGL, LJ Hooker, RACQ, Select Appointments, Unoduo and Vodafone—to name a few.

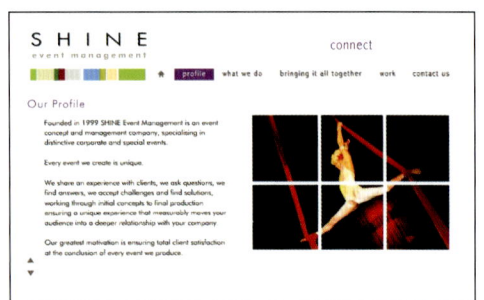

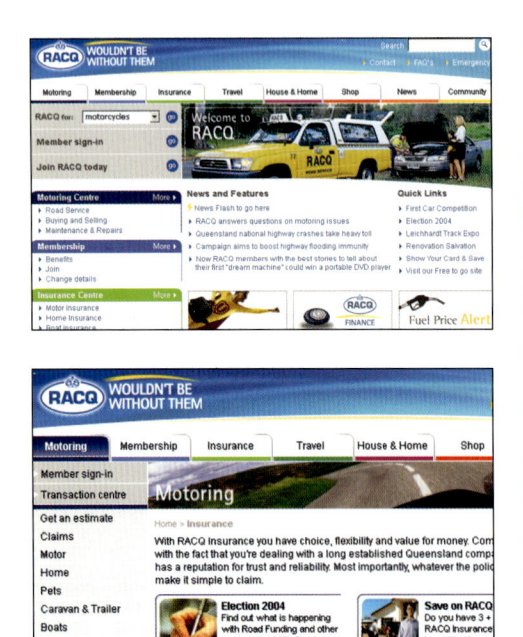

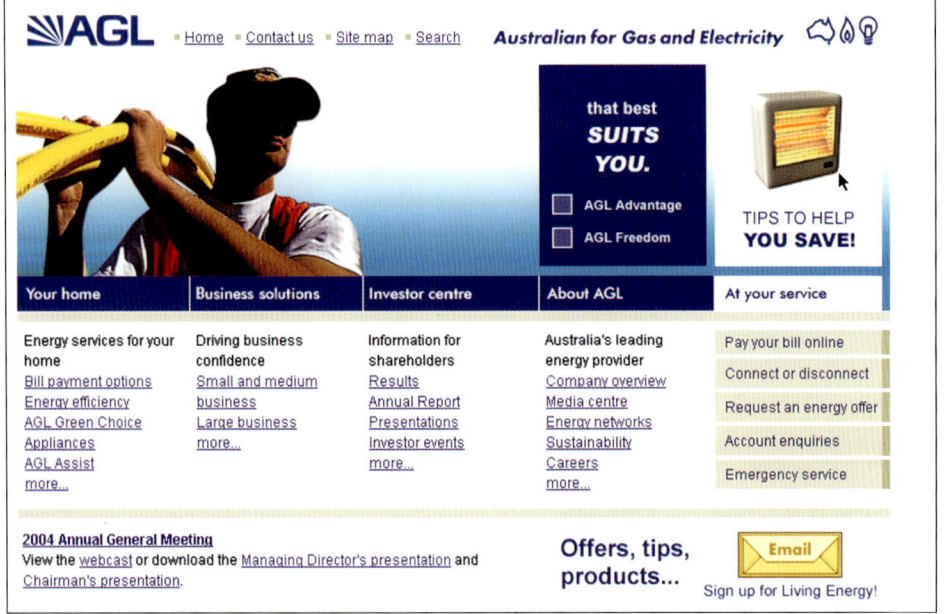

(top left)
Project Website
Client Unoduo

(top right, series)
Project Website
Client Shine Event Management

(above left, series)
Project Website
Client RACQ

(above right)
Project Website
Client AGL

40   Oz Graphix [5]

During a lunch break, Nick's four year old cousin said that Girling Design was the best graphic design business in the universe and that he wanted to work there. Nick replied, 'Thanks mate, with that kind of optimism I want you to be my Client Liaison Manager.' He smiled and replied, 'Do I get to draw pictures with you?'

Girling Design is a specialist graphic and web design firm, striving to produce well formed and effective branding. Nicholas Girling is the creative director, having over ten years design experience.

Girling Design

Suite 108,
89 High Street
Kew VIC 3101

Phone: 03 9854 6166
Mobile: 0418 505 241

www.girlingdesign.com.au
nick@girlingdesign.com.au

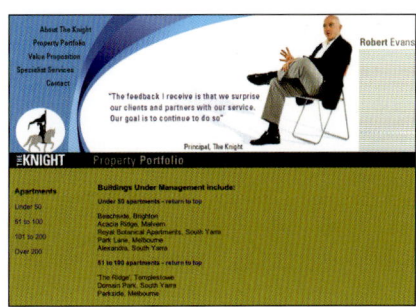

(top left)
Project Brochure spread
Client MJ Printing
Photographer
Lynton Crabb

(logos, top right)
Project Identity designs
Client The Knight
Client RocketRed

(top right centre)
Project Brochure spread
Client MJ Printing

(above left)
Project CMS website
Client DULC Holiday
Cabins Accomodation

(centre right)
Project Website
Client Digital Living
Home Automation

(above right)
Project Website
Client The Knight Body Corporate
Photographer
Andrius Lipsys

Oz Graphix [5]   41

house mouse design

Level 2, 4-10 Bank Place
Melbourne VIC 3000

Phone: 03 9602 5855
Fax: 03 9602 4252

www.housemouse.com.au
mail@housemouse.com.au

house mouse design is a graphic design firm, centrally located in Melbourne's CBD, and has been established since 1996.
The firm employs a team of graphic designers, all sharing the common goal—to communicate effectively and successfully through graphic design.

house mouse design provides a graphic communication service to a range of clients whose output includes annual reports, publications, promotional material, packaging, branding and brochures; and has the resources to steer all projects from original concept to final product.

(top left)
Project Logo design
Client TenderSmart

(top right)
Project Internal HR Program branding
Client Bayer CropScience

(centre)
Project Ministerial Statement
Client Department of Primary Industries

(above)
Project Yarraville Festival campaign
Client Yarraville Festival Committee Inc.

The HSJ Design Group was formed in 1975 and retains the same management today. The group offers copywriting, art direction, design, print management, digital photography, television and radio production, web design and account service.
The group's speciality is photography based catalogues for both trade and consumer, with clients as diverse as mining giant, Rio Tinto, through to retail giant, Nike.

HSJ Design Group

1056 Dandenong Road
Carnegie VIC 3163

Phone: 03 9571 6158
Fax: 03 9571 3993

www.hsj.com.au
ian@hsj.com.au

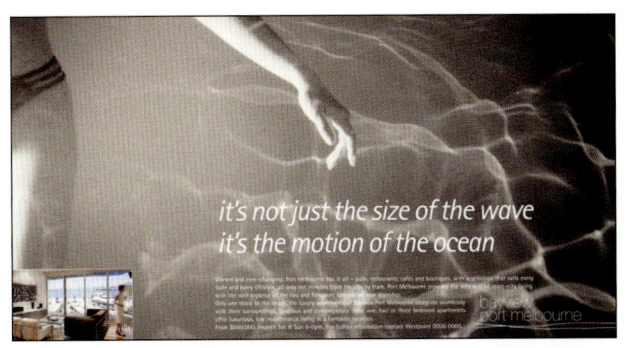

(top left, series)
Project Bayview Apartments
Client Westpoint Corporation

(top right)
Project Yellow brand refresh
Client Yellow Cabs

(above, series)
Project SXY Apartments
Client Baracon Group

Oz Graphix [5]   43

Icon Partners

Level 3, 448 St Kilda Road
Melbourne VIC 3004

Phone: 03 9867 4890
Fax: 03 9867 5890

www.iconpartners.com.au
info@iconpartners.com.au

Icon Partners is a multi disciplined design company with a broad skill base incorporating brand identity, packaging, environmental graphics and print communication. We deliver an integrated approach from research and concept through to product design and market communication. We provide clients with the highest level of quality service by maximising the brand's potential and strategically integrating all levels of visual communication to promote a unified and sound message in the market place.

(top)
Project Brand and redesign of Oak packaging range
Client Wattie's Ltd NZ

(above)
Project Travelan identity campaign, packaging, advertising, promotion and market launch
Client Anadis Limited

44 Oz Graphix [5]

The incorporation of **Icon Raremedia** into our business model enables us to offer a truly 'through the line' seamless solution with digital media design and applications.

See next spread for Icon Raremedia details.

Icon Partners

(top left)
Project Mother's Day catalogue, concept and execution
Client Shaver Shop Australia

(top right)
Project Pasta range packaging
Client Wattie's Ltd NZ

(above)
Project New season product launch campaign, for Sorbent
Client CHH - Consumer Brands/Sorbent

Icon Raremedia

Level 1, 214 Graham Street
Port Melbourne VIC 3207

Phone: 03 9646 2544

www.rare.com.au
info@rare.com.au

With a core focus in design, **Icon Raremedia** specialises in the creation of electronic media that communicates and compels.
We develop customised, effective and innovative solutions to complex communication situations.
Our skills cover the breadth of digital media design and production including internet sites, games, CD-Rom development, multimedia sales presentations and touch screen kiosks.

We have experience with a broad range of clients from global corporations and government agencies to educational institutions, catering to their specific and very individual needs.

(top series)
Project Big Blue Bahamas Incentive website
Client The Business Partnership

(above left)
Project Stamp Collecting Kit Interactive CD with multilevel game
Client iPrint

(above right)
Project Cats & Dogs Stamp Collecting Month website
Client Australia Post

46   Oz Graphix [5]

Icon Raremedia

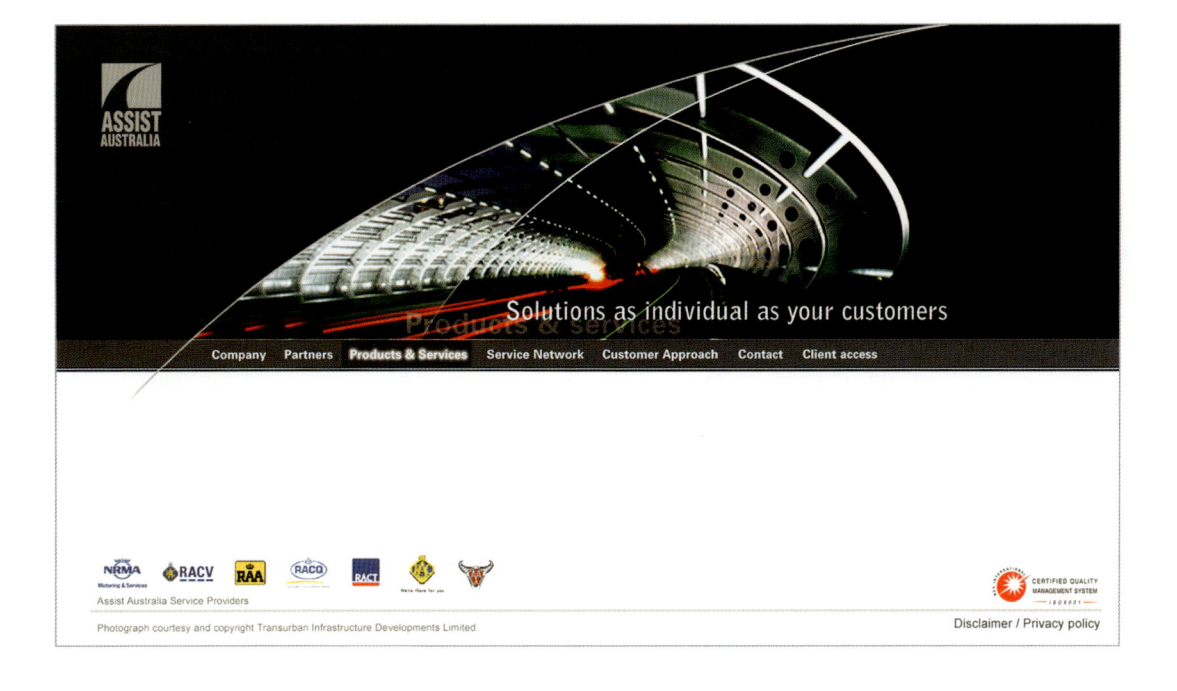

(top)
Project 3 Seller of the Year Incentive CD-Rom
Client The Business Partnership

(above)
Project Corporate website
Client Assist Australia

Ident

Suite 9, Jones Bay Wharf
26-32 Pirrama Road
Pyrmont NSW 2009

Phone: 02 9571 1400
Fax: 02 9571 1250

www.identbrand.com
studio@identbrand.com

Ident is a team of branding specialists who are inspired by creative excellence and motivated by your objectives.
An award winning design consultancy, Ident specialise in branding, corporate identities and packaging. To every project we bring the eyes of enthusiastic consumers and the strategic minds of branding experts.

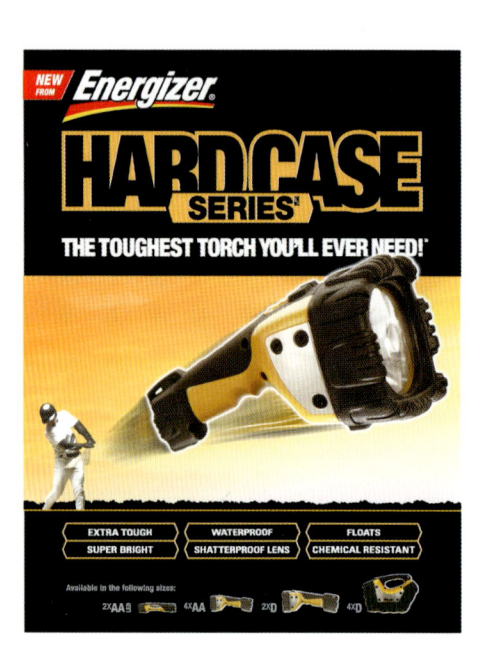

(top left)
Project Rebranding and implementation
Client Equal Opportunity for Women in the Workplace Agency (EOWA)

(top right)
Project Brand identities
Client SAF Property Group
Client MediKwik

(above left)
Project Naming & packaging
Client Avico Electronics

(above right)
Project POS campaign & advertising
Client Energizer

48 Oz Graphix [5]

Ident

(above, series)
Project Branding
Client Sydney Olympic Park Authority

Oz Graphix [5] **49**

Image & Substance

Suite 3, 26 The Parade West
Kent Town SA 5067

Phone: 08 8363 9655
Fax: 08 8363 2120

www.imageandsubstance.com.au
clients@imageandsubstance.com.au

Established in 1995, **Image & Substance** offers specific expertise in both graphic design and website design/construction. The name of our company is symbolic of our determination to provide design services (Image) that clearly reflect an understanding of your business (Substance).

We do not just draw pretty pictures! Image & Substance has a team of young designers who offer a fresh approach to the simple, effective design of logos and stationery, annual reports and corporate publications, exhibition displays, signage, websites and digital design.

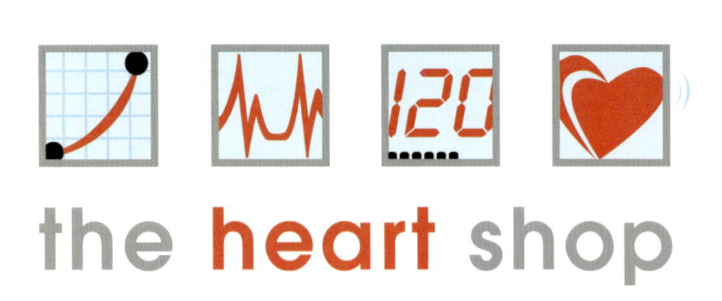

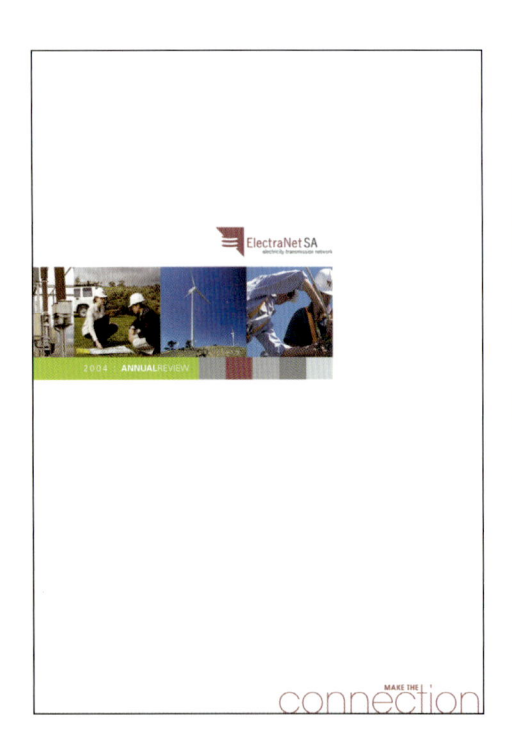

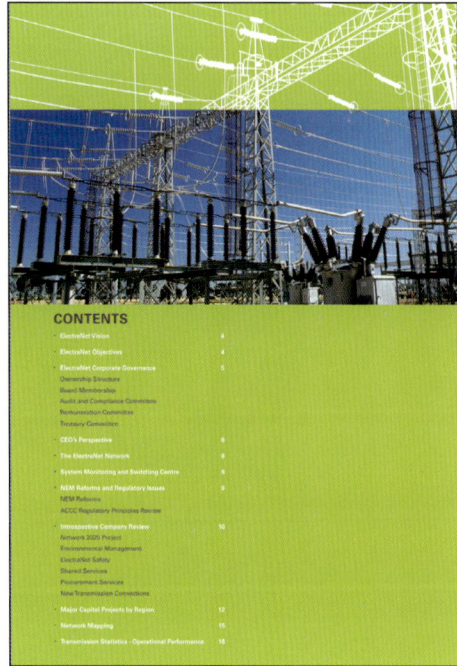

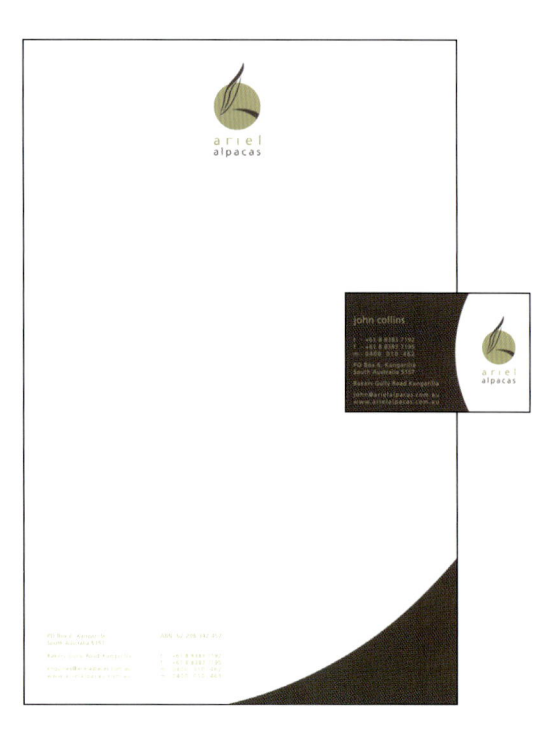

(top left)
Project Corporate identity
Client The Heart Shop

(top right)
Project Corporate identity
Client The Training Factory

(above left & centre)
Project 2004 Annual report
Client ElectraNet SA

(above left)
Project Corporate identity and stationery
Client Ariel Alpacas

50   Oz Graphix [5]

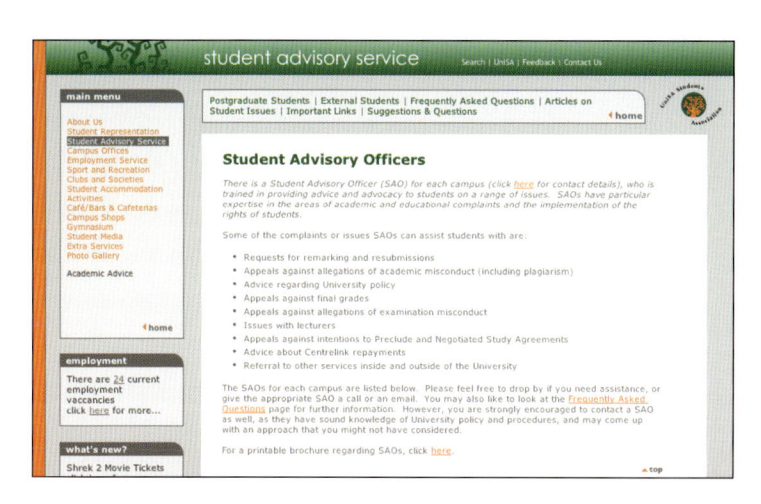

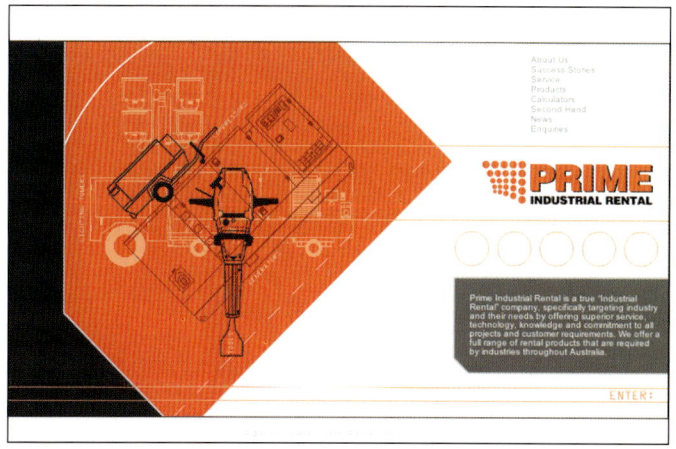

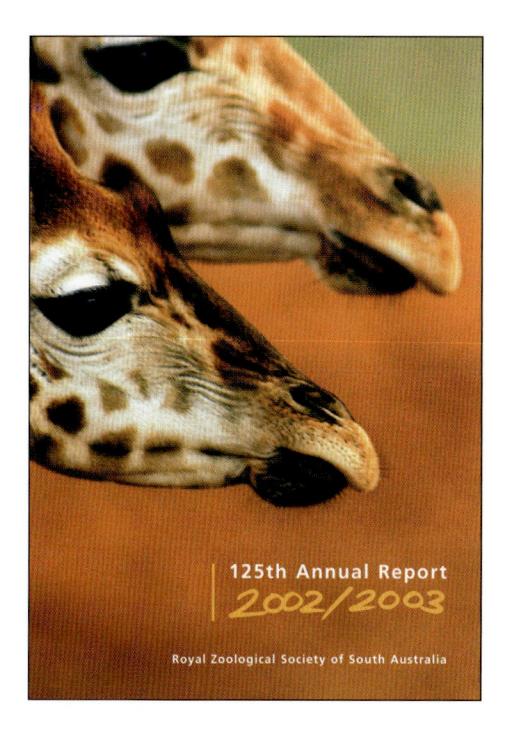

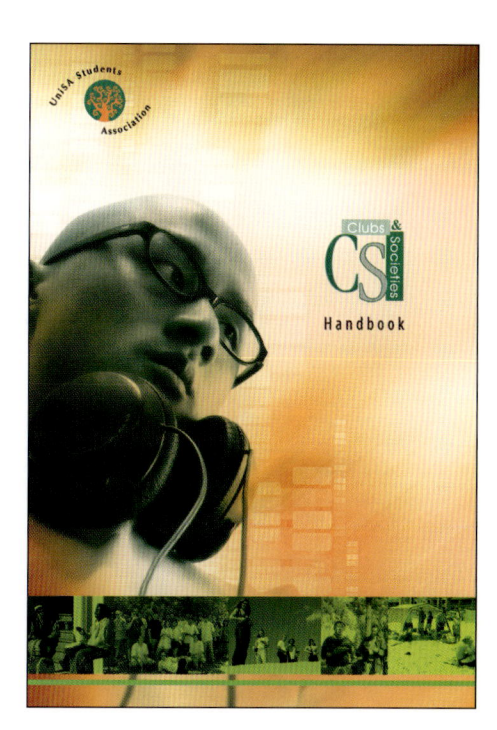

Image & Substance

(top left)
Project Development of new website
Client University of South Australia Students' Association

(top right)
Project Development of new website
Client Prime Industrial Rental

(above left)
Project 2002/2003 Annual report
Client Royal Zoological Society of South Australia

(above centre & right)
Project Clubs & Societies/Sport & Recreation (reversible) Handbook
Client University of South Australia Students' Association

Oz Graphix [5]   51

(top left)
Project Brand identity - image library
Client the Arts Centre

(top right)
Project Brand identity - brandmark
Client the Arts Centre

(above)
Project Packaging - Petit Miam
Client National Foods

(top)
Project Brand identity - environmental graphics
Client Building Commission

(above left)
Project Brand identity - brand books
Client Sensis

(above right)
Project Brand identity - brand book
Client Vividas

Oz Graphix [5]

www.ismgraphicdesign.com.au
ism@ismgraphicdesign.com.au

(top left)
Project New product packaging
Client Lemnos Foods

(top right)
Project Premium packaging launch for National market
Client Ernest Hillier Chocolates

(above left)
Project Branding and packaging for retail market
Client Menora Foods

(above right)
Project National advertising campaign
Client Ernest Hillier Chocolates

54   Oz Graphix [5]

(top left)
Project Premium wine packaging relaunch
Client De Bortoli Wines

(top right)
Project National branding and packaging for food service
Client Coffex Coffee

(above left)
Project National packaging for retail market
Client Jindi Cheese

(above right)
Project Corporate identity and stationery
Client Coffex Coffee

Joseph Casni Design Management

20 Stalwart Street
Prairiewood NSW 2176

Phone: 02 9756 0750
Fax: 02 9604 0160

oneeyedesign@lycos.com

'Creating a viable branded reality that explores and satisfies both the client needs and openly allows for creative visual experimentation are the two fundamental keys needed for effective brand managing.'
Joseph's simple, yet effective philosophy about the exploration of suitable branded identity and management creates a language of style and perception that visually speaks directly to its desired audience.

Project Brand repositioning
The effective repositioning and implementation of cost effective branding to the flagship store through print and environment design

Client Escapade Hair Face Body, Sydney
Photography Thomas Dang

56   Oz Graphix [5]

Joseph Casni Design Management

Latitude Group

7 Phoenix Street
South Yarra VIC 3141

Phone: 03 9826 6199
Fax: 03 9824 2581

www.latitudegroup.com.au
info@latitudegroup.com.au

Latitude is a young creative agency quickly establishing a reputation as a genuine alternative to the major studios with an unmatched combination of services, strategy and fresh thinking. Since appearing on the radar, Latitude has worked on a variety of projects for many businesses from finance to fashion. This way we haven't developed formulae or clichéd ideas about how your project should look or work. Each new client brings a new business approach that demands a new communication approach, which is why we begin with a strategy rather than a favourite colour. At Latitude we share an ambition beyond getting the job done, and believe the true measure of our success rests in the performance of our finished products and the continued satisfaction of our clients. We provide a comprehensive creative service including: all aspects of design, branding, advertising, web, new media, photography and environmental design.

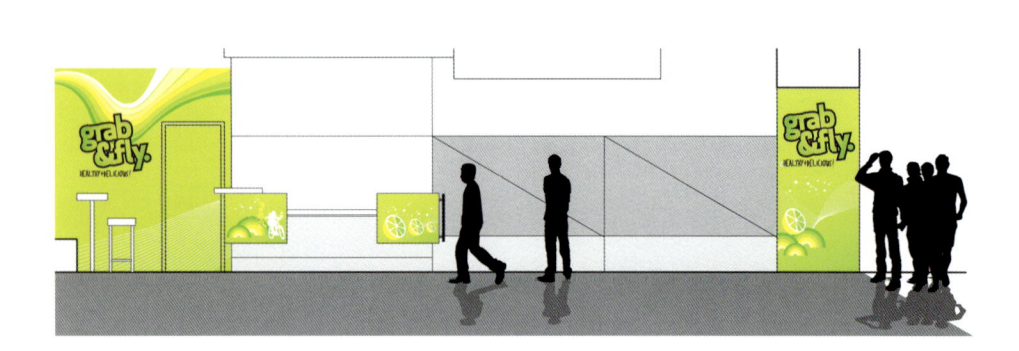

(top left)
Project Naming, branding, collateral, brochure, photography, website
Client Arrivis finance

(top centre)
Project Corporate identity, exhibition stand, media kit, photography
Client International Air Cargo Forum

(top right)
Project Corporate identity, collateral
Client Marmalade Communications

(centre, series)
Project Corporate identity, store graphics, uniforms, packaging, photography
Client Grab'n'fly

(above)
Project Advertising, concepts, promotions, photography
Client Moonee Valley Night Racing

58   Oz Graphix [5]

Latitude Group

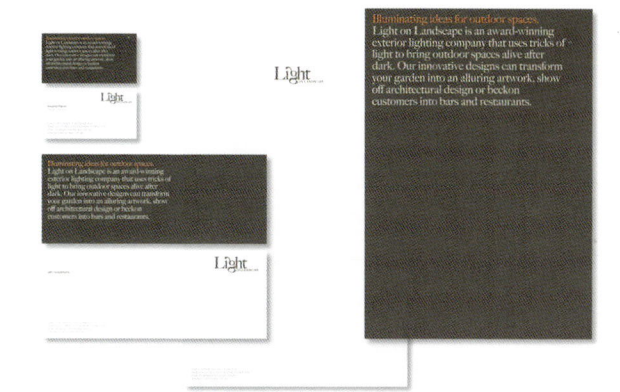

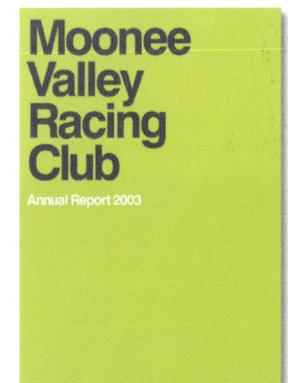

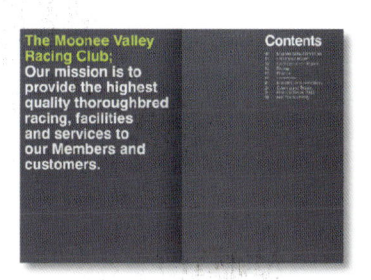

(top, series)
Project Cox Plate advertising and promotions, annual report, photography
Client Moonee Valley

(centre, series)
Project Branding, brochure, photography, store design, website
Client Light on Landscape

(above)
Project Photography
Client Ford Performance Vehicles

Oz Graphix [5]   59

Phone: 07 3875 6191
Fax: 07 3875 6194

www.liveworm.com.au
design@liveworm.com.au

and commercial potential of the college's undergraduate and postgraduate students of design. Successful projects have been completed for clients within the public sector and private enterprise. Liveworm is making design come alive for students and clients alike.

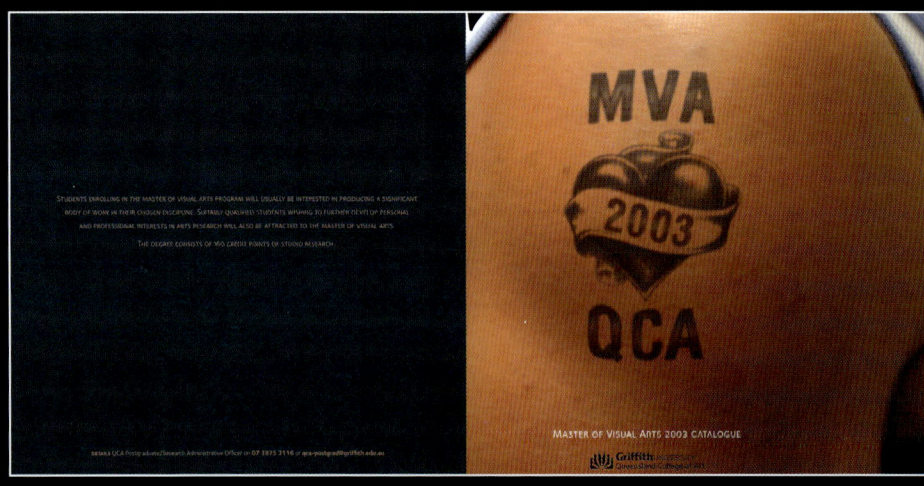

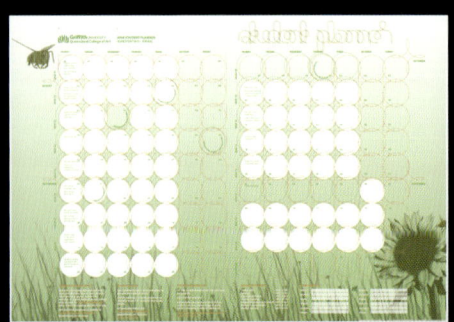

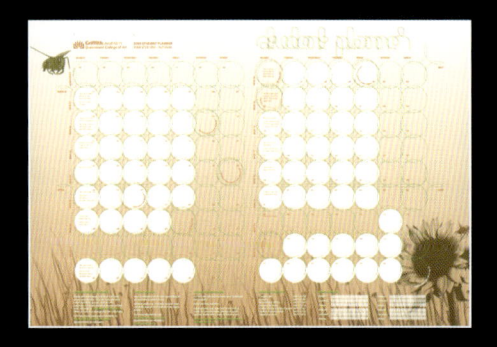

(above left)
Project Poster - Excellence Expo
Client Griffith University

(top right)
Project Exhibition catalogue
Less Ordinary Legends
Client Toowoomba Regional
Art Gallery

(centre right)
Project Exhibition catalogue
MVA Catalogue 2003
Client Queensland College of Art

(above right, series)
Project Student planner
Client Queensland College of Art

Mekanica is a media design business that is grounded in resolving clients' needs with strong creative conceptualisation across the areas of broadcast, interactive, print and exhibition design. The studio focuses on providing challenging design, motion graphics and animation solutions that seamlessly implement brand strategies across all media.

Mekanica

268 Victoria Road
Thornbury VIC 3071

Phone: 03 9484 3578
Fax: 03 9758 4767

www.mekanica.com.au
info@mekanica.com.au

(above)
Project Good Food Guide
video opener
Client The Age

(above)
Project Department of
Infrastructure Trade Mission
Client Immediacy

(above)
Project Salamander Bay Shopping
Centre TVC
Client Bristow Prentice Lambaart Budd

(above)
Project RetailBasics set-up
flash interface
Client MYOB

Oz Graphix [5]   **61**

MDM Design Associates

Melbourne
25 William Street
Richmond VIC 3121

Phone: 03 9429 1177
Fax: 03 9429 9977

Sydney
Level 2, 50 York Street
Sydney NSW 2000

Phone: 1300 761 108
Fax: 02 8243 1122

www.mdmdesign.com.au
mdm@mdmdesign.com.au

MDM Design is a corporate communications firm established over 13 years ago. The company specialises in branding and identity, and in producing investor communication.

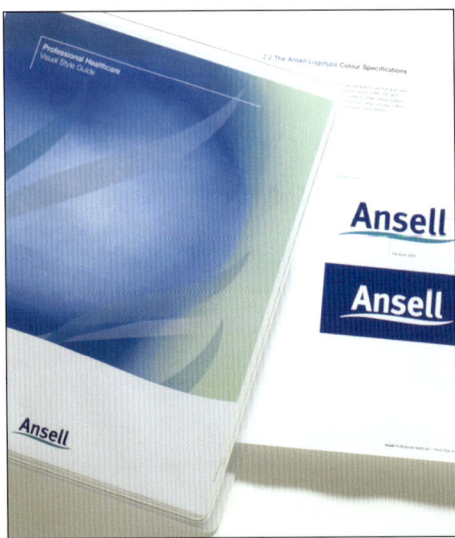

(top left)
Project Visual identity
Client Globe Home Loans

(top centre)
Project Visual identity
Client Acrobatt

(top right)
Project Visual identity
Client Players Own

(above left)
Project Product brochure
Client Pittella

(above centre)
Project Style manual
Client Ansell

(above left)
Project Packaging
Client Rootz

62   Oz Graphix [5]

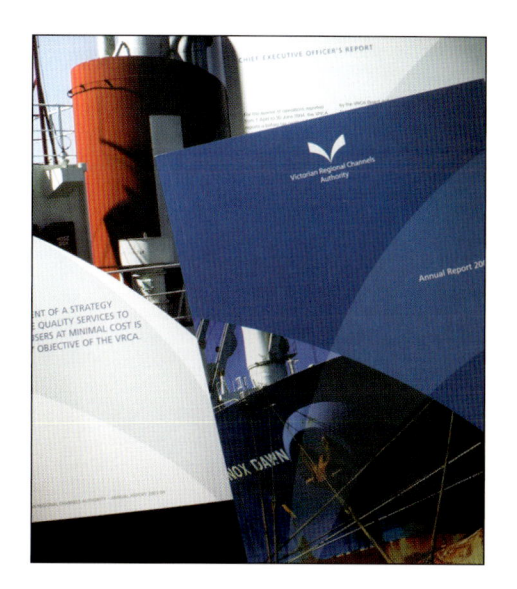

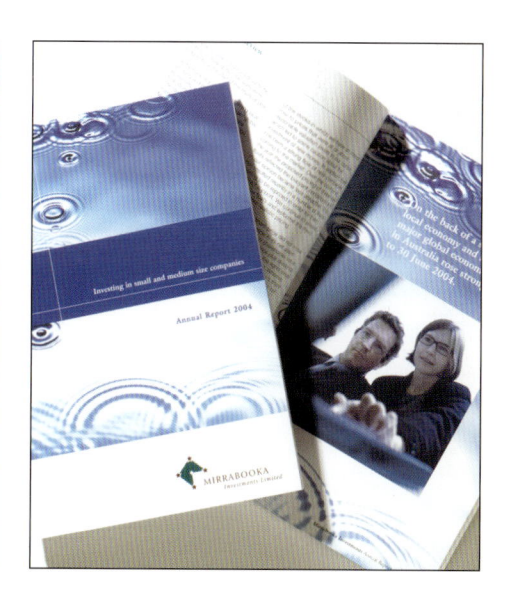

MDM Design Associates

(top left)
Project Annual report
Client Victorian Regional Channels Authority

(top centre)
Project Annual report
Client Department of Human Services

(top left)
Project Environmental report
Client Finsbury Green Printing

(above left)
Project Annual report
Client Willmott Forests

(above centre)
Project Annual report
Client McPherson's Limited

(above right)
Project Annual report
Client Mirrabooka Investments

Oz Graphix [5] **63**

Moon Design

38 Boronia Street
Redfern East NSW 2016

Phone: 02 9690 2999
Fax: 02 9698 0576

www.moondesign.com.au
mail@moondesign.com.au

Moon is a Sydney-based strategic branding, communications and design agency with an international reputation for excellence. Creative as well as effective, the agency continues to set new standards through campaigns that fuse together the traditional disciplines of design, advertising and branding—with proven results.

This award-winning agency has built an enviable reputation through a wide and varied client list including Qantas, Sydney Symphony, Sydney Theatre Company, Hutchison 3, Orange, Seafolly, Trent Nathan, Van Heusen, Jetstar and Nike

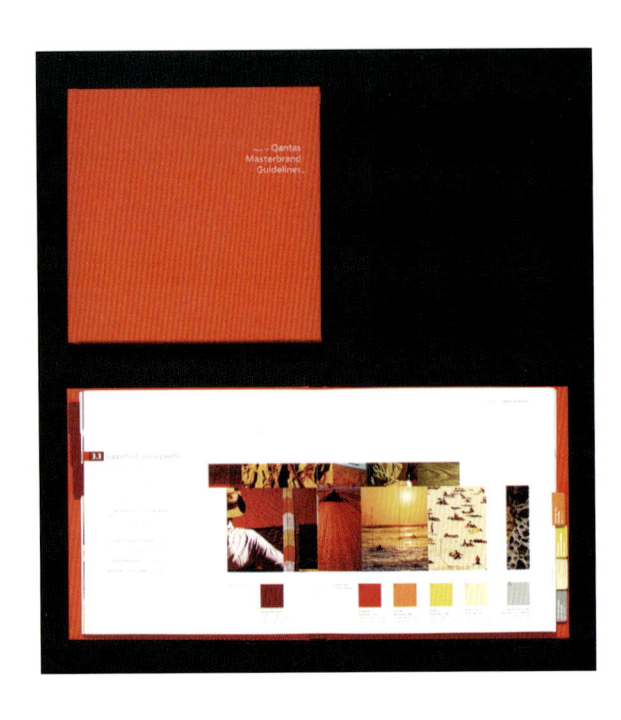

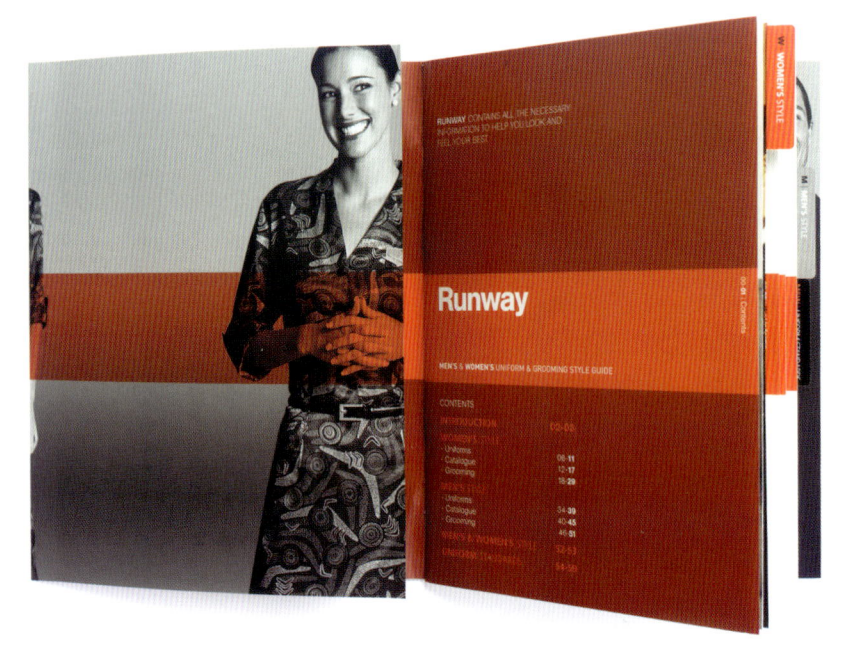

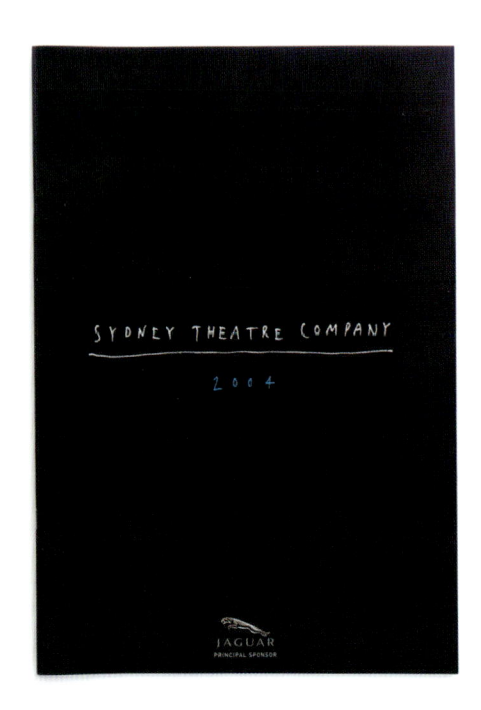

(top left)
Project Qantas Masterbrand Guidelines
Client Qantas

(top right)
Project Qantas Runway Uniform Guidelines
Client Qantas

(above)
Project Sydney Theatre Company 2004 Subscription brochure
Client Sydney Theatre Company

Moon Design

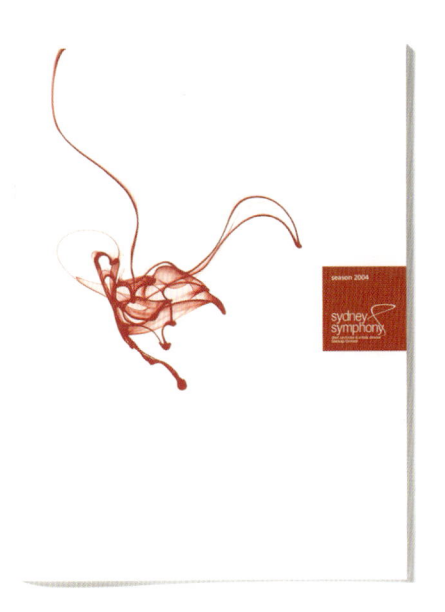

(this page, series)
Project Sydney Symphony Season 2004
Client Sydney Symphony

Oz Graphix [5] **65**

Monitor Graphics

Level 1/1A Yarra Street
South Yarra VIC 3141

Phone: 03 9826 8744
Fax: 03 9826 8544

www.monitorgraphics.com.au
design@monitorgraphics.com.au

Design studio **Monitor Graphics** has worked with some of Australia's most recognised brands to produce materials that are unique, appropriate and inspiring. With an emphasis on the Arts and a dynamic team of multi-disciplined designers, cutting-edge technology and creative expertise, Monitor Graphics offers cost efficiency, service excellence and results that deliver. From print based advertising, corporate identities and multimedia productions, to packaging, licensed product and website design, Monitor Graphics offers complete end-to-end design and marketing solutions.

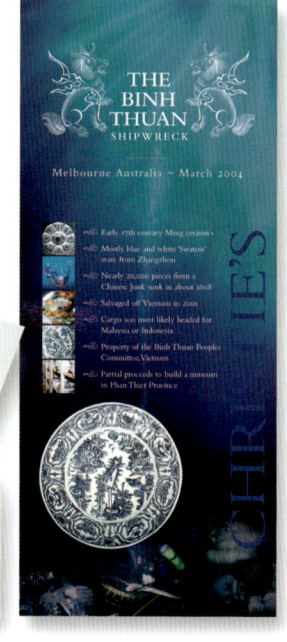

(top left)
Project Australian Superbike Championship logo
Client Motorcycling Australia

(top right)
Project The Binh Thuan Shipwreck catalogue and poster
Client Christie's Australia

(above)
Project Self promotional CD-Rom
Client Australian Contemporary Aboriginal Art

Percept Creative Group aim to listen, understand and improve the public perception of the businesses they work with. This is done by exciting themselves and their clients about a brand's personality, and then developing design solutions that trigger the desired market response.

Their goal is to enjoy all client relationships—delivering service and product that ensure the experience is positive—and to share in the delight of each project's outcome and its benefit to that business.

Percept Creative Group

PO Box 189
Cronulla NSW 2230

Phone: 02 9544 3200
Fax: 02 9544 5600

www.percept.com.au
lewis@percept.com.au

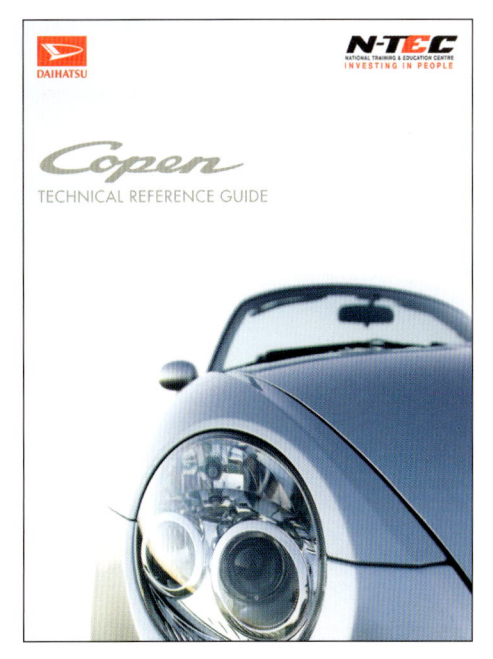

(top, logos left to right)
Project Corporate identities
Client Aquius
Client Ireland Global
Client Teamspace

(top right)
Project Poster design 2004
Client Johnson's Kids
Wakakirri

(centre right)
Project Knorr brand packaging
Client Unilever

(above left)
Project Technical reference manual
Client Daihatsu

(above right)
Project Double page advertisement
Client SMP

Oz Graphix [5] 67

PhD

52 Ourimbah Road
Mosman NSW 2088

Phone: 02 9968 4022
Fax: 02 9968 4822

www.phdcreative.net
studio@pacifichighway.net

PhD provides strategic planning and design solutions to corporate and marketing management. Our focus is to develop powerful expressions for your brand and create business value and growth.
• Strategic planning
• Corporate & brand development
• Packaging
• Retail visual communications
• Print communications
• Web design & development

(above)
Project i-tag
Identity development for launch of trial cashless payment system for McDonald's drive-thru
Client The Transurban Group and McDonald's Australia
Photography Courtesy of Christian Mushenko

68   Oz Graphix [5]

(above)
Project McDonald's packaging design
Revitalising the McDonald's brand across
all packaging
Client McDonald's Australia
Photography Courtesy of Christian Mushenko

Plutonium

Level 1, 332-342 Lorimer Street
Port Melbourne VIC 3207

Phone: 03 9684 1247
Fax: 03 9684 1206

www.dpa.com.au
peter@dpa.com.au
stuart@dpa.com.au

Plutonium is a Melbourne based design agency dedicated to providing effective creative solutions. They have a strong focus on generating dynamic communication, an open working environment and strong client relationships.

Armed with a team of multi-disciplined designers, state of the art technology and creative expertise, Plutonium promotes and nurtures a creative language and intelligence rarely found in today's design society.

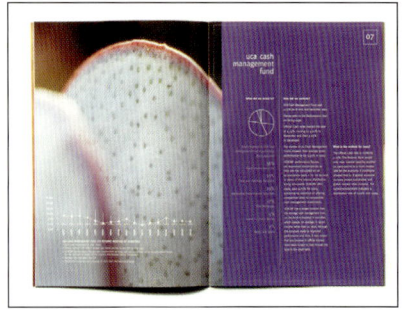

(top, series)
Project Annual report
Client Victoria Police
Photography Stuart Black

(above, series)
Project Annual report
Client UCA Funds Management
Photography Peter Buchholz

70   Oz Graphix [5]

Plutonium

(top, series)
Project Oz Child campaign
(annual report, identity, letterhead, cards)
Client Oz Child
Photography Grant Hobson

(above left)
Project RSPCA 'Ban Duck-Shooting' campaign
(media kit, brochure, postcard, poster)
Client RSPCA
Photography Paul Muir

(above right, top to bottom)
Project Corporate identity programs
Client Oz Child, BSA, Scope

Oz Graphix [5] 71

Rokat Design

Suite A, Level 1
520 Dorset Road
Croydon South VIC 3136

Phone: 03 9725 7316
Fax: 03 9725 2114

www.rokatdesign.com.au
info@rokatdesign.com.au

Understanding that design plays an integral part in the image of all businesses, **Rokat Design** is committed to creating unique, original and innovative solutions to any visual communication challenge. Rokat will take you on a smooth ride from research, brainstorming and initial concept designs through to printing, production or web publishing, ensuring that you are kept informed and in control throughout the entire trip. Great design fuels Rokat, and a passion to create only the best for businesses, large or small, ensures that every project will be fresh, unique and tailored to your needs or corporate image.

Rokat creates corporate identities, promotional material, book covers, packaging, posters, websites and any design project imaginable. Let your business blast off with Rokat.

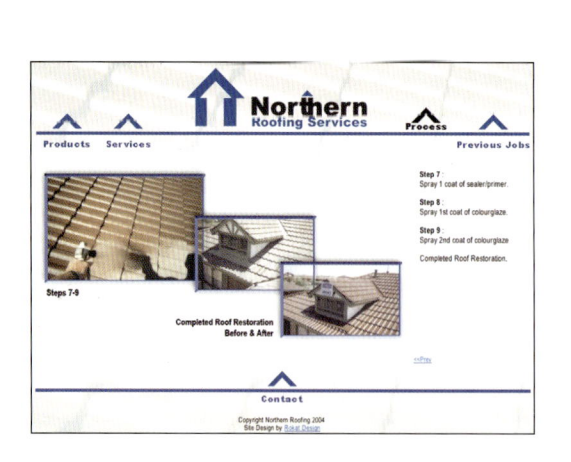

(top left)
Project Corporate identity
Client Audio Tours

(top right)
Project Corporate identity
Client Rokat Design

(centre left)
Project Book cover & interior
Client Scripture Union

(above left)
Project Logo & website design
Client Northern Roofing

(above right)
Project Promotional material
Client The Salvation Army Men's Bible Convention

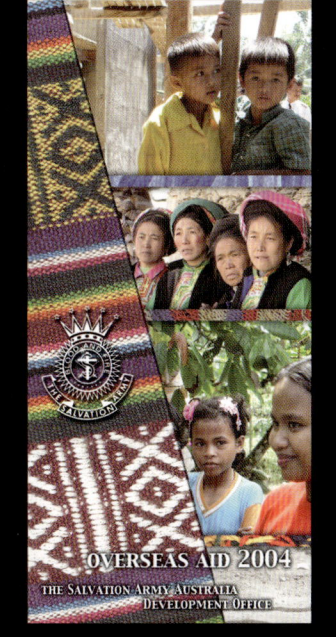

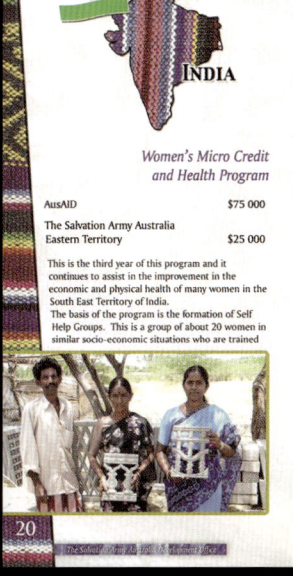

(top left)
Project Book cover
Client Scripture Union

(top right)
Project Annual report
Client The Salvation Army Australia Development Office

(above, series)
Project Corporate brochure
Client Internet Vision Technologies

Oz Graphix [5] 73

RPBrown

Studio 11, 156 Parramatta Road
Camperdown NSW 2050

Phone: 02 9557 9078
Fax: 02 9557 9079

www.rpbrown.com
mrbrown@rpbrown.com

RPBrown produces ideas that turn heads. Mr Brown's approach to advertising and design is a seamless blend of concept and visual, to produce memorable communication and brand consistency across all mediums.

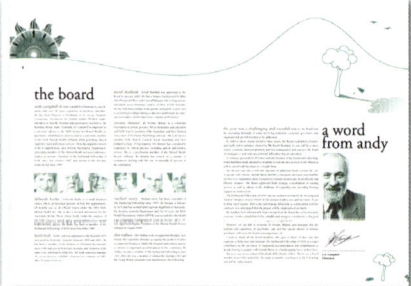

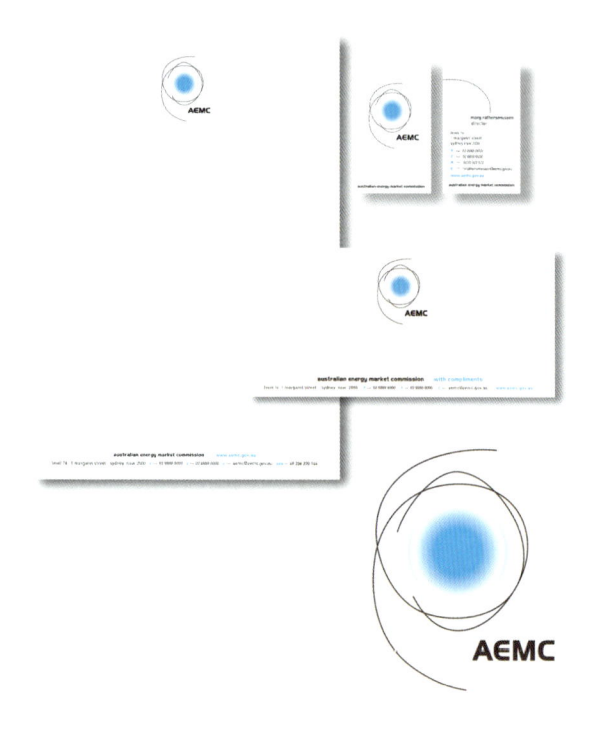

(top left, series)
Project Branding and image - promotional material including logo, folder and stationery.
Client Express Glass

(top right)
Project Branding and image - logo and stationery
Client Australian Energy Market Commission

(centre left)
Project Annual report 2003
Client The Richmond Fellowship of NSW

(above)
Project Print advertisements - concept, copywriting and images
Client NRMA Touring Services

74   Oz Graphix [5]

Simon Bowden Design drives to create a dynamic and striking concept for all our clients, while keeping their objective at the forefront of the design process.

Simon Bowden Design
(SB+D)

Level 1
176 Burgundy Street
Heidelberg VIC 3084

Phone: 03 9458 2844
Fax: 03 9458 3877

www.sbdesign.net.au
info@sbdesign.net.au

(top left)
Project The Beaumonde has been designed to promote a range of childrens socks and hosiery
Clients Goonderra

(top right)
Project Corporate identity
Client Allens Estate Agents

(logos centre, left to right)
Project Corporate identities
Client Gridiron Victoria
Client Melbourne Special Beverages
Client Embrace Health Club

Client Manufacturing & Engineering Skills Advisory Body Victoria
Client Summit Management Solutions
Client The Clearance Store

Show & Tell Creative

Level 5, Studio 10
365 Little Collins Street
Melbourne VIC 3000

Phone: 03 8676 0366
Fax: 03 9670 2508

www.showandtell.com.au
studio@showandtell.com.au

Located in the heart of Melbourne's CBD, **Show & Tell** is a dynamic design group providing creative outcomes in the areas of:

- Corporate identity development
- Stationery and marketing collateral
- Websites and content management
- Exhibition and display design

Our strategic approach ensures we deliver brilliant solutions for our clients where all areas of marketing and design reflect the style unique to each client's business.

See what we have for show and tell today.

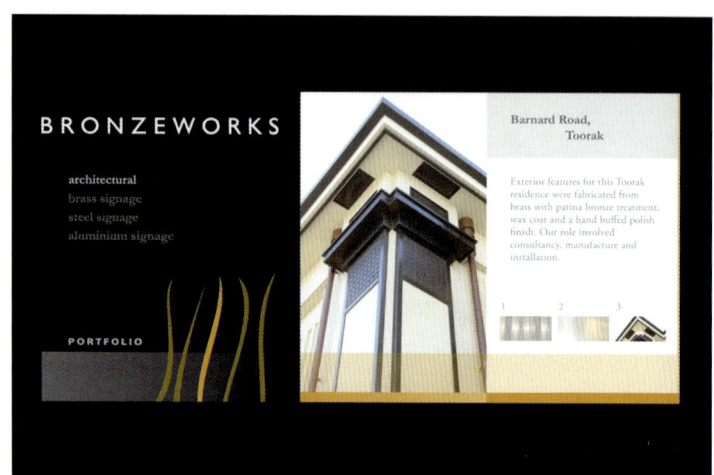

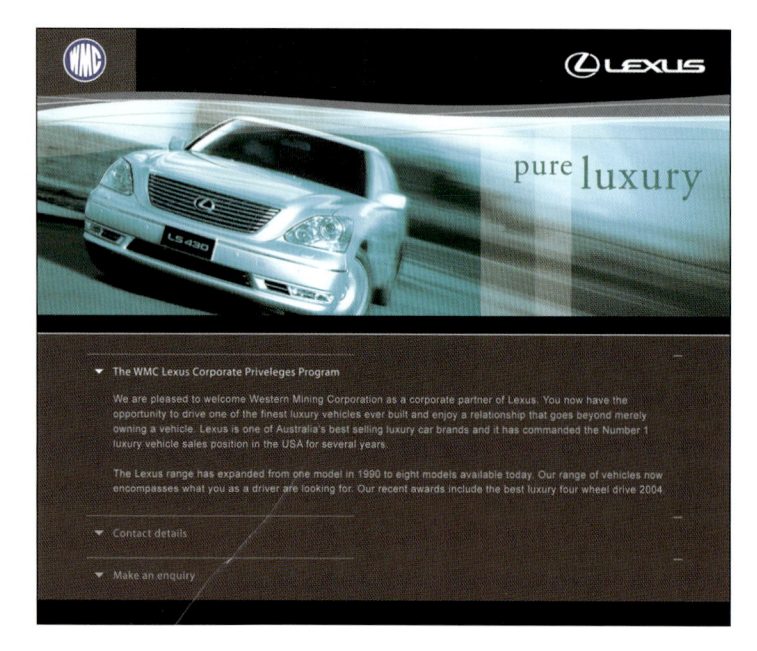

(top left)
Project Website and content management system for launching the Sureshot GPS golfing product
www.tee2greengps.com
Client Tee2Green Technologies

(top right)
Project Flash website for showcasing specialist metal finishes
www.bronzeworks.com.au
Client Bronzeworks

(above left)
Project Corporate intranet micro site for Western Mining Corporation
Client Lexus of Brighton

(above right)
Project Website for Vikki Leigh Martin's sewing classes
www.sewingclasses.com.au
Client Vikki Leigh Martin

Show & Tell Creative

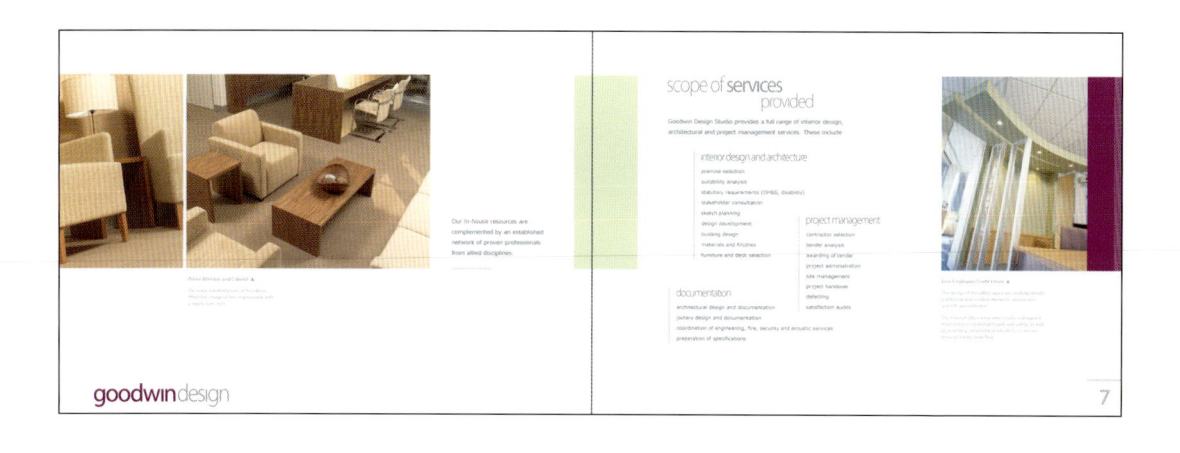

(top left)
Project Exhibition stand design to launch Virgin Atlantic's upper class
Client HPL United Kingdom

(above left)
Project Corporate brochure design
Client Goodwin Design Studio

(logos, top to bottom)
Project Corporate identities
Client Ashley Institute of Training
Client Newlands Upholstery
Client Wettowel

Oz Graphix [5] **77**

Sprout Creative

Tiki Building
55 Hudson Fysh Avenue
Parap NT 0820

Phone: 08 8980 5700
Fax: 08 8980 5701

www.sprout.com.au
info@sprout.com.au

Sprout Creative specialises in professional graphic design, multimedia, displays and websites. With a young and energetic design team based in Darwin, Sprout develops highly effective communication material from concept to campaigns and across-the-board media applications.

Sprout prides itself on its originality and its understanding of context and environment. Sprout Creative's client base includes private and public organisations, and it is widely recognised as a leader of the creative industry in the Northern Territory.

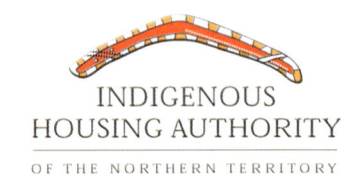

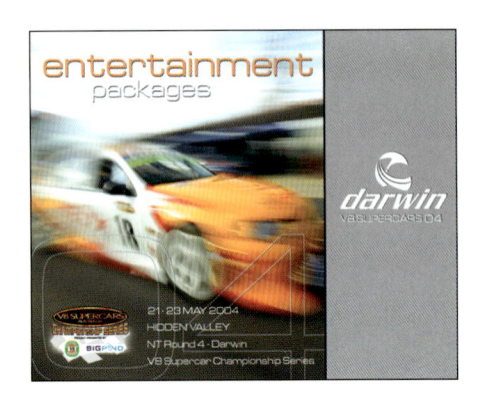

(top left, logo)
Project The Territory marketing campaign
Client Northern Territory Government

(top centre left, logo)
Project NT Round - V8 Supercar Championship Series 2004
Client NT Major Events Company

(top centre right, logo)
Project 25 years self-government
Client NT Major Events Company

(top right, logo)
Project Corporate identity
Client Indigenous Housing Authority of the Northern Territory

(centre)
Project Entertainment packages, NT Round - V8 Supercar Championship Series 2004
Client NT Major Events Company

(above, series)
Project International course guide
Client Charles Darwin University

78   Oz Graphix [5]

(top left)
Project Unique and Boutique Campaign
Client Northern Territory Tourist Commission

(top centre)
Project Annual report
Client Australasia Railway Corporation

(top right)
Project Environment report
Client Power and Water Corporation

(above left)
Project Origins magazine
Client Charles Darwin University

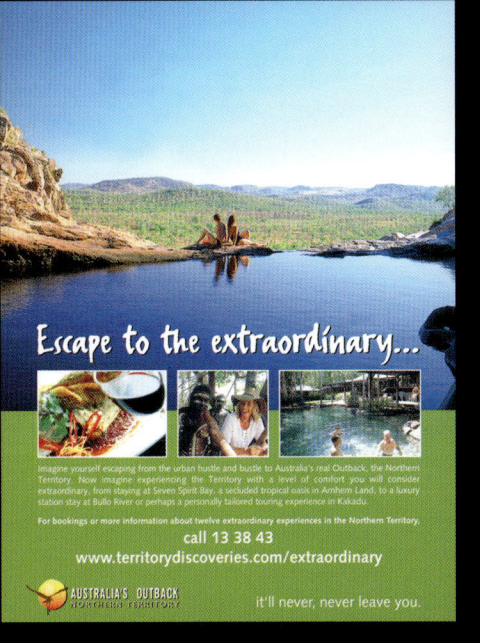

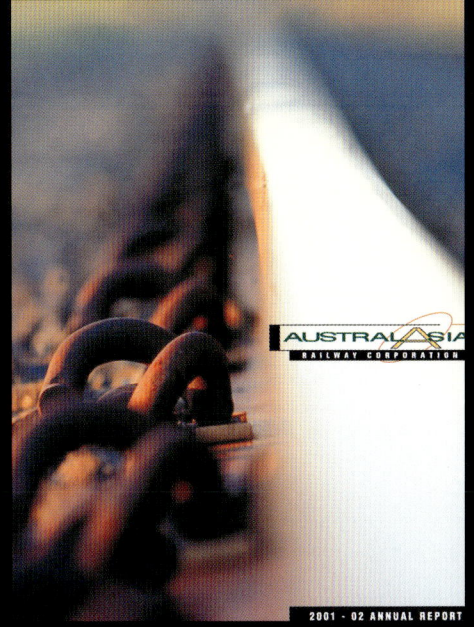

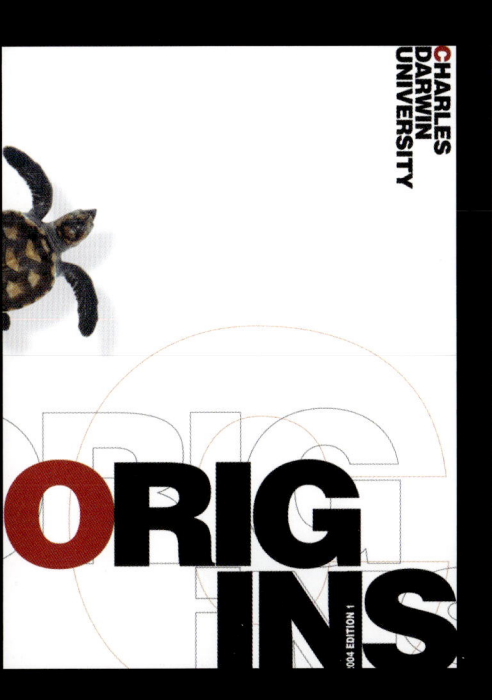

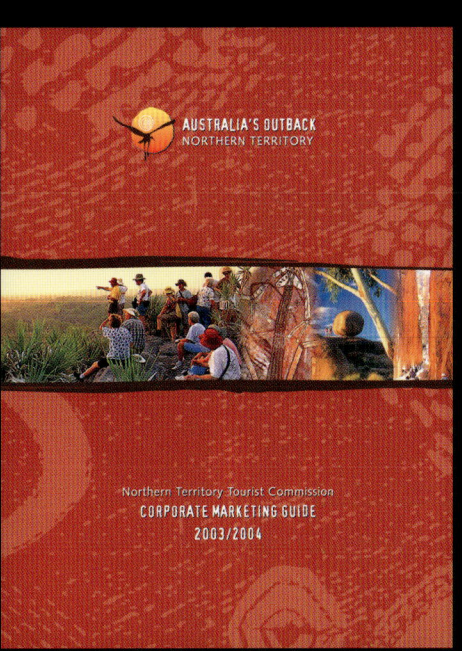

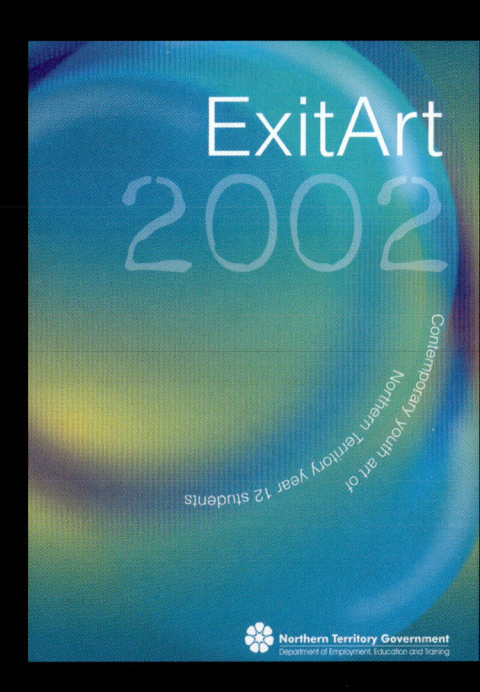

(above centre)
Project Corporate branding suite
Client Northern Territory Tourist Commission

(above right)
Project ExitArt exhibition catalogue
Client NT Department of Employment, Education and Training

Oz Graphix [5] **79**

Studio Equator

Level 1, 225 Chapel Street
Prahran VIC 3181

Phone: 03 9510 8855
Fax: 03 9510 0188

www.studioequator.com
design@studioequator.com

Studio Equator harbours a collective group of young forward thinking designers who thrive on challenges. Offering a fresh approach and energetic level of experimentation, we act as an extension to our clients' business, cultivating their objectives together with our experiences, resulting in powerful communication and branding messages.

Diversity and growth is our objective, design is our speciality. We provide integrated disciplines within:
• Graphic Design—corporate identity & branding, environmental graphics & signage, publication, packaging, print, advertising design, web design,
• Interior Design—hospitality, fashion, retail, specialty shops and franchises.

(top, series)
Project Rebranding and packaging
Client Gold Star Food Processing

(above left)
Project Interior fitout and identity design
Client Whiskee Blue Bar

(above right)
Project Interior fitout and identity design
Client R4 café

80   Oz Graphix [5]

Studio Equator

(top, logos left to right)
Project Identity design
Client Sakura House
Client Tilkah Fashion
Client Ideal Shade Solutions
Client Sustain Industries
Client Blahnik restaurant
Client Alter it clothing alterations

(above left)
Project Index interior design publication
Client RMIT University

(above right)
Project CD single
Client Jimmy Barnes & Gary Pinto

Oz Graphix [5] **81**

Studio218

PO Box 2143
Dickson ACT 2606

Phone: 02 6247 0059
Fax: 02 6249 7373

www.studio218.com.au
info@studio218.com.au

Studio218 is a Canberra based design studio. It successfully supplies fresh and innovative solutions to clients design and communication needs. Formerly known as Green Words & Images, Studio218 has wide experience in both private and public sectors and all areas of digital and print media. Studio218 specialises in publications, branding, corporate identity and websites from concept development to final design.

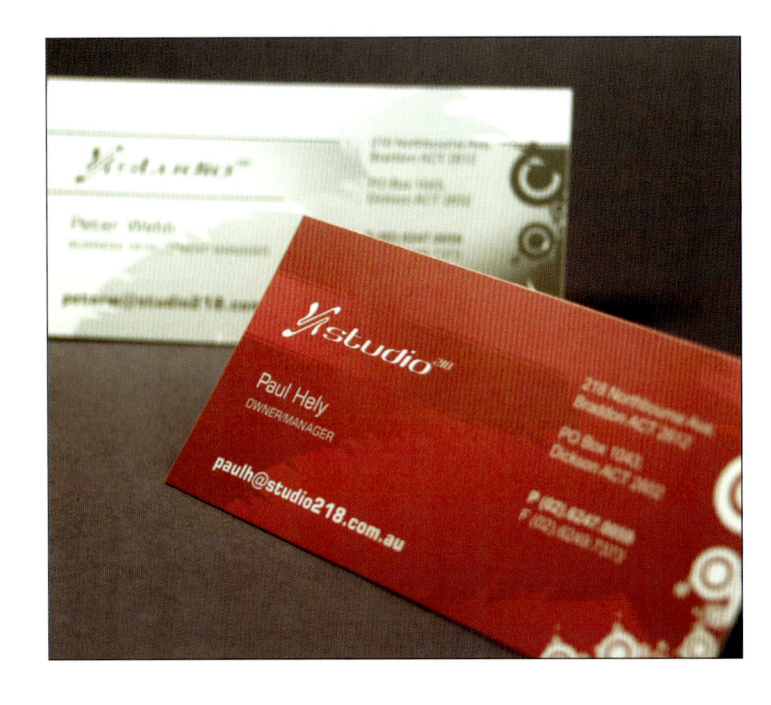

(top left)
Project Business cards & stationery
Formerly GWi, Studio218 needed a new 'look' to go with their new name and new approach to design
Client Self promotion

(top right)
Project Crime prevention kit for small business, farm crime
Client Attorney-General's Department

(above left)
Project Hand-out flyers to promote new 'cellar door' weekend jazz festivals
Client The Kamberra Wine company

(above right)
Project Invitation for fundraising dinner party, Gourmet in the gardens
Client Mental Health research

82   Oz Graphix [5]

Storm Creative is a tenacious Sydney based creative agency riding a new wave. They have a passion for design, and focus on delivering top-notch creative, multimedia and web design. The Storm Creative philosophy is to do away with heavy advertising agency style infrastructure, keep business simple and employ highly creative experienced designers. This mix has seen Storm Creative experience continued success since its inception in 2000.

When dealing with Storm Creative, clients deal directly with one designer from concept to completion, ensuring that designs are carried through efficiently (without the Chinese Whispers phenomenon) and the final product is reproduced to the standards that the designer intended. Brainstorming, regular creative meetings and office sports are all essential ingredients.

Storm Creative

Level 4, 8 West Street
North Sydney NSW 2060

Phone: 02 9922 1011
Fax: 02 9922 1444

www.stormcreative.com.au
mail@stormcreative.com.au

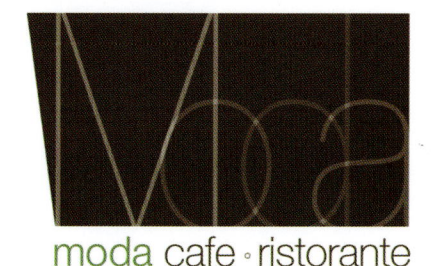

(top left)
Project Product launch brochure
Client Maytag Australia

(top right)
Project Arai Helmets posters
Client Cassons

(centre left)
Project Cocktail booklet
Client Suntory Australia

(centre right)
Project Company profile
Client Primary Health Care Limited

(above left)
Project Momo's corporate identity
Client San Marco Group

(above right)
Project Moda corporate identity
Client San Marco Group

Oz Graphix [5]   **83**

The Graphic Image Studio

6 Bastow Place
Mulgrave VIC 3170

Phone: 03 9562 1920
Fax: 03 9562 2585

www.tgis.com.au
studio@tgis.com.au

The Graphic Image Studio is an internationally recognised, award winning design studio specialising in architectural/interior design publications, corporate identity and packaging design. Established in 1989 and based in Melbourne, the team shares the vision of strong communication in print, producing high quality brochures, point-of-sale material and reports.

Displaying a unique talent for theatrical promotion, the studio's work has featured in Hong Kong, Singapore, South Africa and the UK, as significant events tour the world.

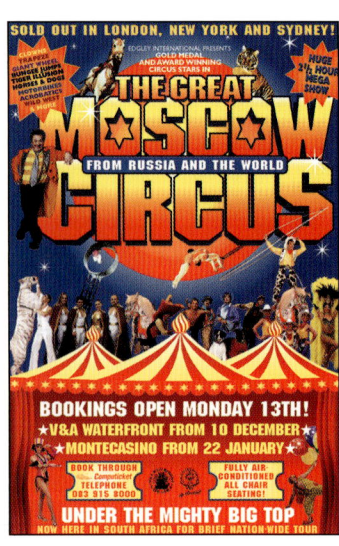

(top left)
Project Full colour publications for world-wide distribution
Client The Images Publishing Group

(top right)
Project Logos
Client TFC Australia Pty Ltd
Client West Rock Farm Conference Centre

(above left)
Project Various packaging
Client TFC Australia Pty Ltd

(above right)
Project The Great Moscow Circus, South African Tour
Client Edgley International

84 Oz Graphix [5]

Tracey Allen is a graphic designer, photographer and educator. For the past six years she has lectured at the University of Tasmania and the University of Technology, Sydney. Tracey established the student design studio at the University of Tasmania and has received several design awards. Tracey remains committed to her own design practice that includes corporate identity, publication and book design.

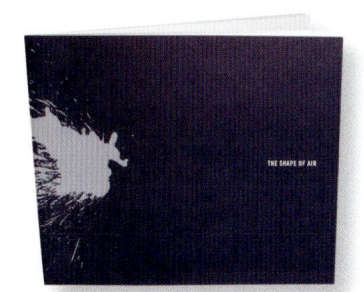

Tracey Allen

PO Box 71
Ellendale TAS 7140

Mobile: 0408 207 270

www.traceyallen.com
tcallen@bigpond.com

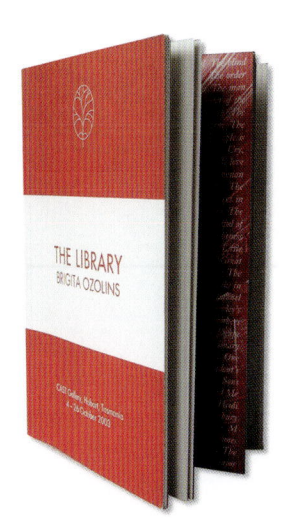

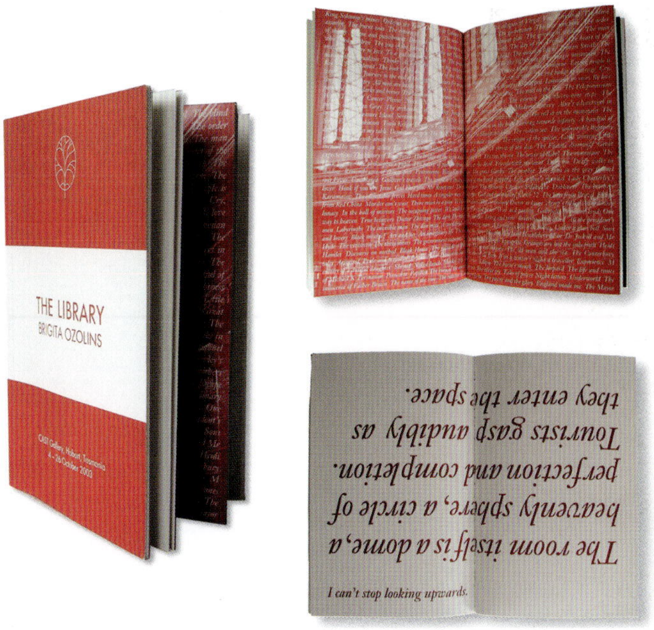

(top left)
Project Exhibition catalogues 'Shape of Air', 'Sequence'
Client Plimsoll Gallery and Carnegie Gallery

(top right)
Project Corporate identities
Client Noyce Legal, Connery & Partners Lawyers and Broadcam

(above left)
Project New Social Commentaries 'Boundaries'
Client Warrnambool Art Gallery Award 2004

(above right)
Project Exhibition catalogue 'The Library'
Client Contemporary Art Services Tasmania and Brigita Ozolins

Triple 888 Studios

81-83 Wigram Street
Parramatta NSW 2150

Phone: 02 9891 2888
Fax: 02 9891 1283

www.triple888.com.au
designit@triple888.com.au

Triple 888 Studios provide creative artwork services of the highest standards with meticulous attention to detail, showcasing each client's products in the best way possible and creating long lasting partnerships. Established in 1986, the studio has grown to provide creative design and strategic marketing services. Our strong design team has produced many award winning solutions—from packaging, brochures, corporate images, websites and advertisements. As a successful business, our services are employed by local and international clientele operating in a wide range of industries, including pharmaceutical, automotive, homewares, industrial, cosmetics and consumables.

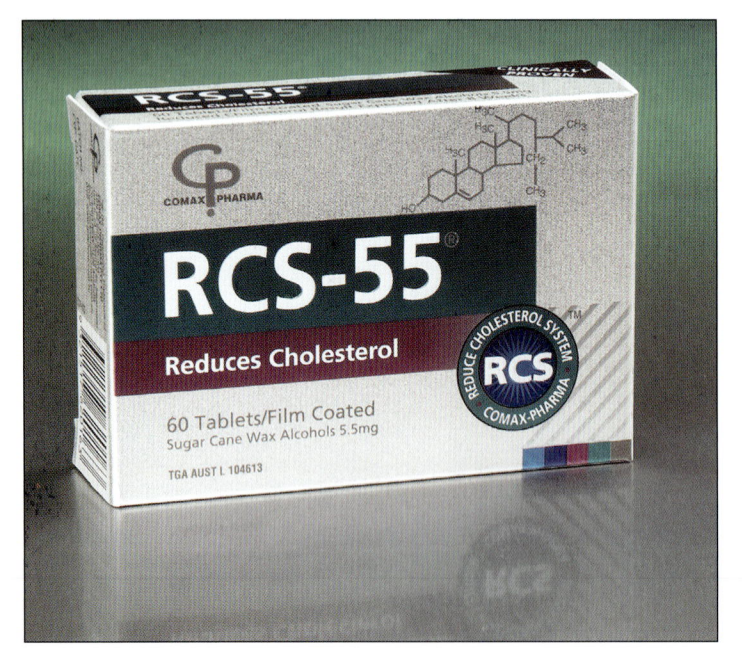

(logos, top left)
Project Brand identities
Client Premier Fruit & Vegetables
Client The Original Diet
Client Trend Realty

(top right)
Project V8X knife block
Client Sheldon and Hammond

(above left)
Project RCS-55
Client Comax Pharma

(above right)
Project Le Sock bottle holder
Client Sheldon and Hammond

86   Oz Graphix [5]

Established in 1986, **Visible Ink Design** is a unique, award winning design studio highly regarded for its originality and quick response. From initial discussion through concept and design development, the studio prides itself on its close liaison with its clients at every stage of the process. Visible Ink's creative designs ensure an end product that goes beyond our client's expectations. Visible Ink specialises mainly in entertainment graphics, having packaged over 40 stage productions over the past six years. We're a design company small enough to respond quickly to a client's needs, but also large enough with the in-house facilities to manage the most comprehensive projects.

Visible Ink Design

Suite 5A, 4-6 Duke Street
Windsor VIC 3181

Phone: 03 9510 7455
Fax: 03 9510 4866

www.visibleink.com.au
visibleink@bigpond.com

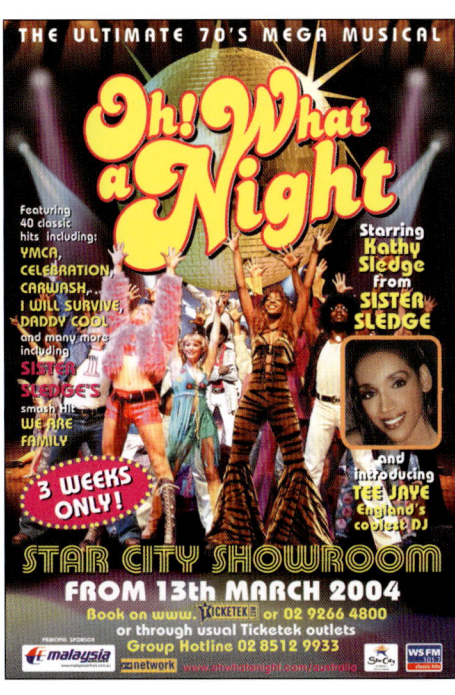

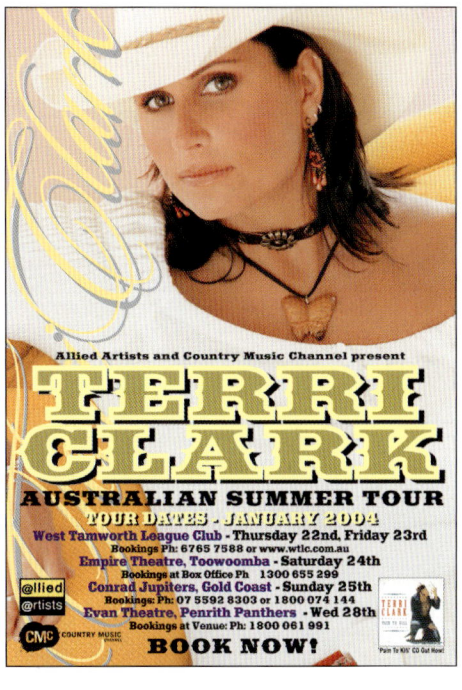

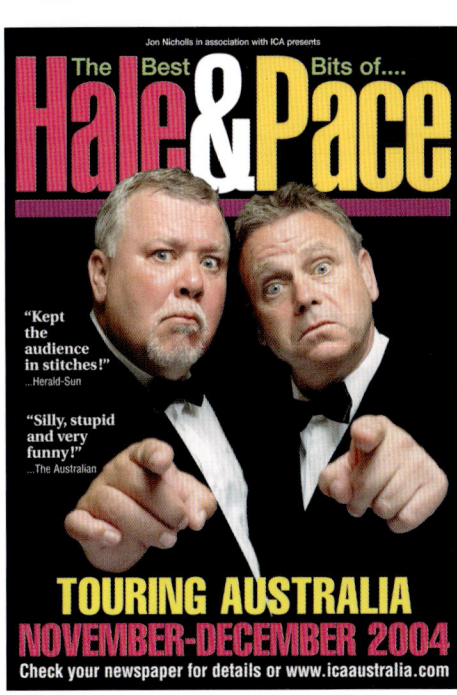

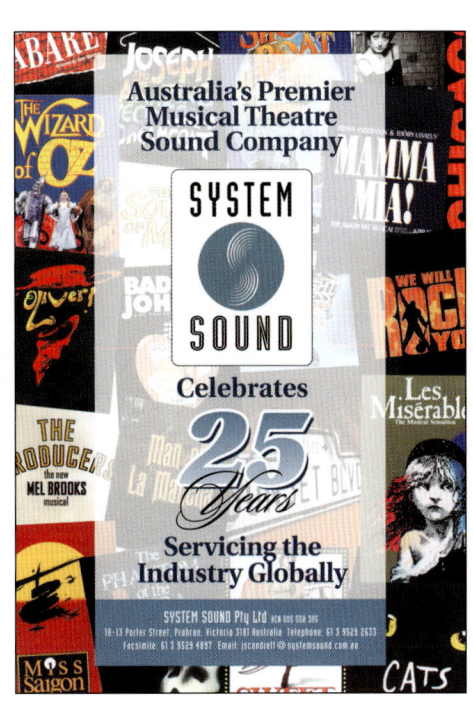

(top left)
Project It's a Dad Thing! Comedy stage production Logo, total design package & tour support
Client TML Enterprises

(top centre)
Project Oh! What a Night - The 70's disco musical Logo & total design package
Client Jon Nicholls Productions

(top right)
Project Project Terri Clark - Australian Tour Logo, total design package & tour support
Client Allied Artists

(above left)
Project Hale & Pace - Australasian Tour Logo, design package & tour support
Client Jon Nicholls Prod & ICA

(above centre)
Project System Sound - Musical Theatre Sound Company 25th Anniversary design package
Client System Sound

(above right)
Project The Mark Twain You Don't Know - stage production Logo & total design package
Client Olentangy Music

Oz Graphix [5] **87**

Underline: Fitch

Level 11, 35 Clarence Street
Sydney NSW 2000

Phone: 02 9778 7474
Fax: 02 9778 7555

www.underline-fitch.com
info@underline-fitch.com

A multi discipline design consultancy providing Industrial, Interior and Graphic design through a network of studios in the Asia Pacific Region— Sydney, Singapore, Kuala Lumpur, Ho Chi Minh and Hong Kong through to China— **Underline: Fitch** provides a strategic approach to taking brands into the 'third dimension' of the retail environment.

From the simplest expression of brand through packaging form and graphics to merchandising and creating the total retail environment, Underline: Fitch operates as the Asia Pacific arm of Fitch Global Studios. This ensures our designs reflect global trends while delivering innovative solutions to lead the local market.

(logos, top to bottom)
Project Corporate identities
Client fetchmemovies
Client The Committee for Sydney
Client Armidale Dumaresq Council

(top right)
Project Corporate
brochure & price guide
Client McWilliams Wines

(above right)
Project Brochure celebrating
15 years of pro bono work
Client Gilbert + Tobin Lawyers

88   Oz Graphix [5]

touch point.
Based on this belief we have developed our consultancy over 25 years of operation to ensure our design and production capability can deliver on this principal.

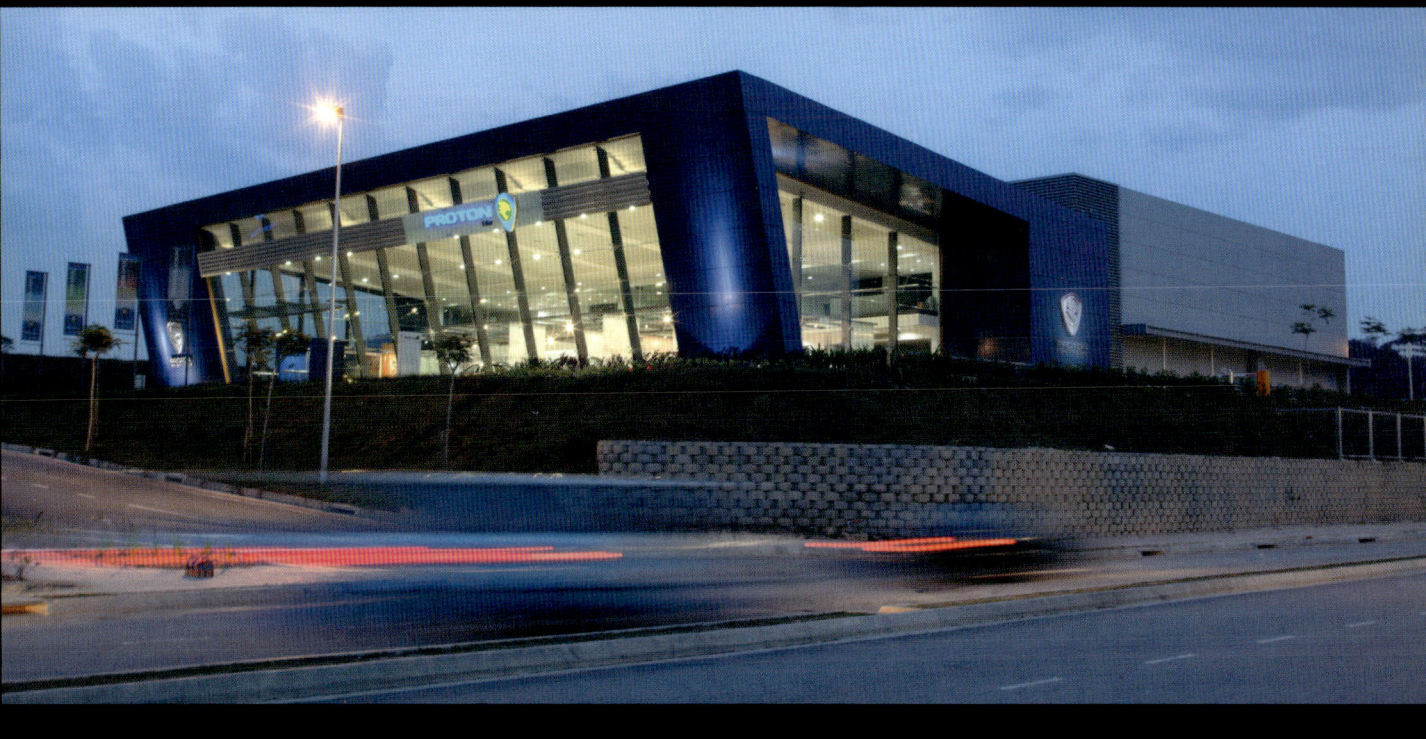

(top)
Project Iconic Architecture for Proton's flagship showroom
Client Proton

(above left)
Project The interior design based on the customer path delivers individual model attributes in a dynamic way through retail theatre
Client Proton

(centre right)
Project Proton's Malaysian landscape heritage is reflected within the customer lounges
Client Proton

(above right)
Project Night sees the Primary Proton Pylon gently morph into a series of predetermined colours, through the innovative use of transparent panels
Client Proton

Underline: Fitch

Level 11, 35 Clarence Street
Sydney NSW 2000

Phone: 02 9778 7474
Fax: 02 9778 7555

www.underline-fitch.com
info@underline-fitch.com

The ability of **Underline: Fitch** to work across a diverse and challenging range of projects, covering a broad geographic area, through our Asia Pacific network locally and the Fitch network globally, makes our consultancy the ideal choice for corporate identity or retail implementation programs.

(top left)
Project Design and documentation of the interior fit out
Client Heineken:
'Ministry Of Sound' Bar Taiwan

(top right)
Project Backlit bar front with contemporary barcode striping
Client Heineken:
'Ministry Of Sound' Bar Taiwan

(above left)
Project Unique use of Heineken logo in glass to create a coffee table ice tub for product sampling
Client Heineken:
'Ministry Of Sound' Bar Taiwan

(above right)
Project Frosted green glass for subtle softening of Heineken bottle display
Client Heineken:
'Ministry Of Sound' Bar Taiwan

Underline: Fitch is skilled in concept presentation through our ability to present high definition virtual reality 3D modelling of product, packaging or environment.
This style of presentation is available in either static or animated form as a virtual work around or walk through.

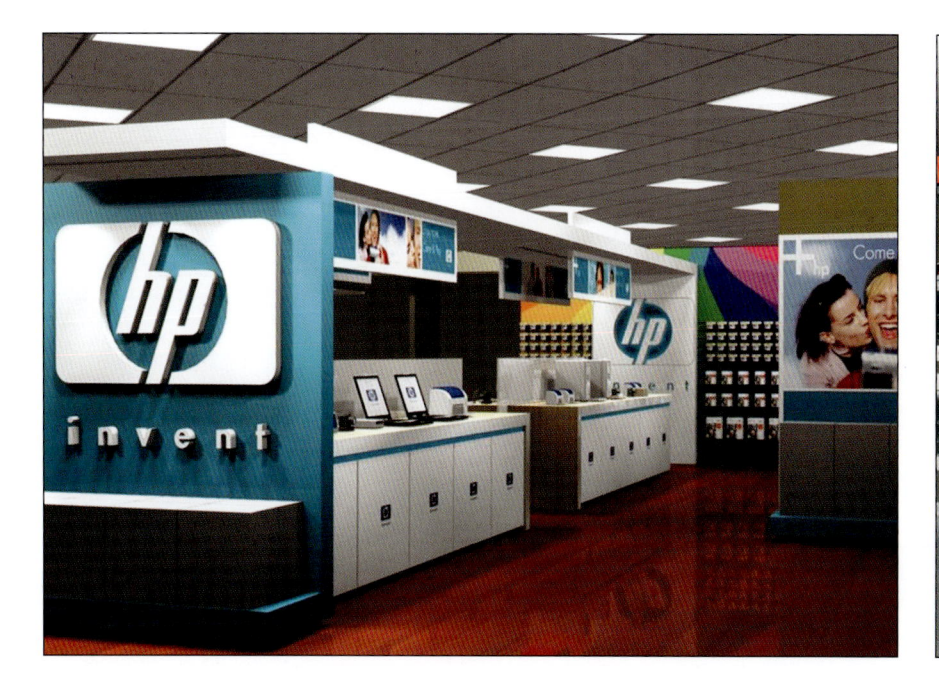

Underline: Fitch

(top)
Project 3D modelling of design for Nokia Concept Store, Bangkapi Thailand
Client Nokia

(above left)
Project The design and 3D modelling of 'Digital Imaging' retail environment
Client Hewlett-Packard

(above right)
Project The design and 3D modelling of 'Home Products Selection Centers' for the retail environment
Client Electrolux

Oz Graphix [5] 91

Oz Graphix [5]

ILLUSTRATORS

Bill Wood Illustration

24 Goold Street
Burwood VIC 3125

Phone: 03 9888 0011
Fax: 03 9833 4577

www.illustration.com.au
billwood@illustration.com.au

Is Communication important to you? **Bill Wood Illustration** has been in the business of communication in Australia and overseas since 1988. With a small but dedicated team of three, we employ a wide range of styles and techniques to suit a variety of projects.
Our diverse range of clients hail from the fields of advertising, design, packaging, direct marketing and publishing.
Keeping a low profile when promoting our work, Bill Wood Illustration prefers the reliable, but tested positive word-of-mouth approach, allowing us to maintain a loyal regular customer base.

(top)
Project Walled city image
The Walled Royal palace for the satirical travel book 'Phaic Tan'
Client Working Dog

(above left)
Project New icon for Solo can
Studio Davidson Design
Client Cadbury Schweppes

(above centre)
Project Commemorative coin - the King & Queen of Phaic Tan
Client Working Dog

(above right)
Project Golf-tee tin
An exclusive tin box for Golf tees purchased through mail order only
Client Harry Day

94   Oz Graphix [5]

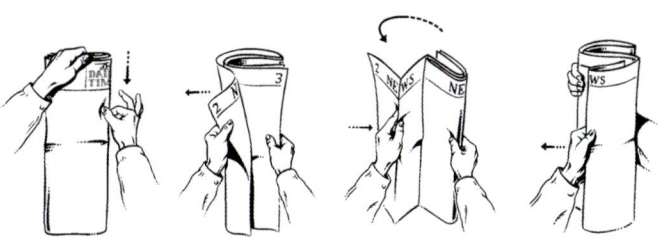

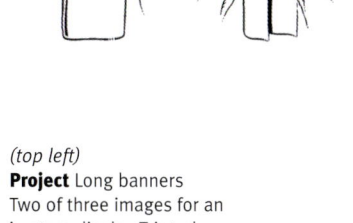

Bill Wood Illustration

(top left)
Project Long banners
Two of three images for an
in-store display Triptych
Studio Ektavo design
Client Laurent French patisserie

(top right)
Project Yoga poses
Traditional Phaic Tan Yoga positions
Client Working Dog

(above left)
Project Instructional icons for
folding a broadsheet newspaper
from a book - 'The Uncyclopedia'
Client The Text Publishing Company

(above right)
Project Man on bucking horse -
poster for an in-store promotion
Studio Wilson Everard
Client Hard Yakka

Oz Graphix [5] 95

D MAX

1 Pinewood Drive
Mount Waverley VIC 3149

Phone: 03 9803 5804
Fax: 03 9803 5814

www.dmaxpl.com.au
chris@dmaxpl.com.au

D MAX has produced an extensive range of illustrations for a variety of clients in the design, advertising and publishing industries. All of these illustrations have been produced using a combination of LightWave and Photoshop.

Chris Hughes established D MAX over ten years ago and provides a range of design, advertising, illustration, 3D, website design, CD Rom and television/video services.

Design to the MAX!

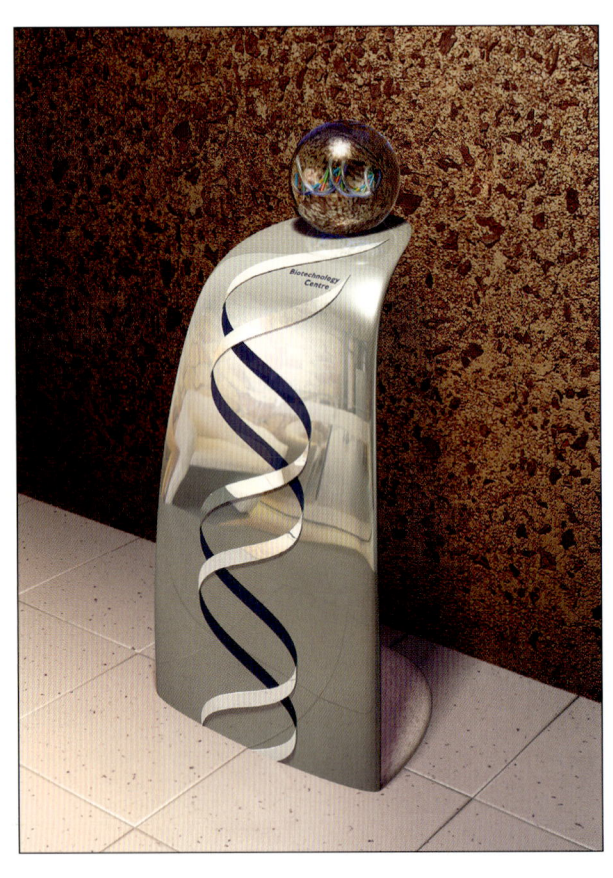

(top left)
Project Computer generated visual for a commemorative sculpture
Client The Walter and Eliza Hall Institute of Medical Research

(above right)
Project Space fantasy book cover design
Client D MAX

(above)
Project Telstra Store tugboat
Client Clemenger/Telstra

Deborah Niland is a freelance artist and illustrator. She has a special interest in children's books and has a list of successful titles to her name. In addition she has illustrated for a variety of publications, newspapers and magazines. In her work, Deborah employs different styles—traditional and digital. She particularly enjoys illustrating stories that are humorous and character based, with pigs and hippos being definite favourites!

Deborah Niland

Phone: 02 9460 7442
Fax: 02 9460 7443

www.deborah-niland.com.au
d.niland@bigpond.net.au

(top left)
Project Alien
Client Artist's portfolio

(top right)
Project My Hippopotamus is on our Caravan Roof getting Sunburnt
Client Hodder Children's Books

(above left)
Project Sea dragon
Client Artist's portfolio

(above right)
Project Mother's Day
Client Artist's portfolio

Dee Texidor - Illustrator and Designer

'Narraburra'
1907 Deer Vale Road
Deer Vale NSW 2453

Phone: 02 6657 3355
Mobile: 0417 859 105

deetexidor.com
dee@texidor.com

Dee Texidor has worked in Graphic design and illustration for 17 years in marketing and publishing.
Following two years as an inhouse designer and illustrator for Scholastic Australia, Dee began her foray into freelance illustration.
Dee's first children's picture/novelty book 'Tiny Turtles' (2001) for The Book Company has gone into reprint several times, and she has created over 30 books since.
Clients include Dolly, Total Girl, For Me, Women's Weekly magazine, New Frontier, Scholastic, Blake Education, Thomson Learning, Ice Water Press and Children's Book Council.
She enjoys working in bright watercolours, pastels and digital illustration.

(top left)
Project Icons
Client Ice Water Press

(top right)
Project Little girl

(above left)
Project Lois Ladybird

(above right)
Project Dusty & Shaggy

Type doublehappy.net into your web browser and you half expect an Adults Only warning and a barrage of 'Barely Legal' pop-ups. Instead, you arrive safe and warm in illustrator, Dane Flighty's world of unique characters and flash animations. Dane's illustrations have appeared in IDN and Australian Financial Review's 'Boss' magazine—to name a few.

Double Happy

1/19 Lyndhurst Crescent
Hawthorn VIC 3122

Phone: 03 9819 0586
Mobile: 0400 188 170

www.doublehappy.net
info@doublehappy.net

(above)
Project Operation Aloha
Client Self promotion

James Hart Design

PO Box 817
Mornington VIC 3931

Mobile: 0403 722 211

www.jameshart.com.au
info@jameshart.com.au

James Hart Design is an illustration and design studio based on the Mornington Peninsula, near Melbourne.
James Hart is a digital and traditional illustrator focused on providing creative solutions for companies seeking identification, advertising, graphic art, concept development, character design and visualisation across all media.

James was raise on animated TV shows of the 80s, video games and comics. His passion for character design and the human condition has helped him produce illustrations for clients including: John Wiley & Sons, UC Publishing and Mercury Mobility.

(top left)
Project English Alive cover
Client John Wiley & Sons Australia

(top right)
Project Educational illustration for English text book
Client John Wiley & Sons Australia

(above left)
Project Educational reading book cover
Client UC Publishing

(above right)
Project Educational illustration for Japanese language book
Client John Wiley & Sons Australia

James Hart Design

(top left)
Project Visual Deception
Client Self promotional

(top centre)
Project Akeldama
Client Noise 2003

(top right)
Project Educational illustration for English text book
Client John Wiley & Sons Australia

(above left)
Project X Men
Client Self promotional

(above right)
Project Bad Droid
Client Self promotional

Oz Graphix [5] 101

Ian F Faulkner and Associates

44 Riverview Road
Clareville NSW 2107

Phone: 02 9973 1928
Fax: 02 9973 3221

www.ianfaulknerillustrator.com
iffaulk@ozemail.com.au

As an illustrator, cartographer and cartoonist, I am always trying to present information in as informative and interesting manner as possible. Please visit my website for more varied samples of my work.

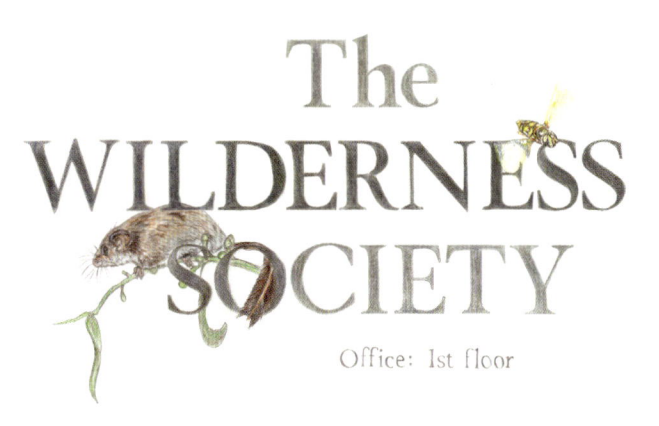

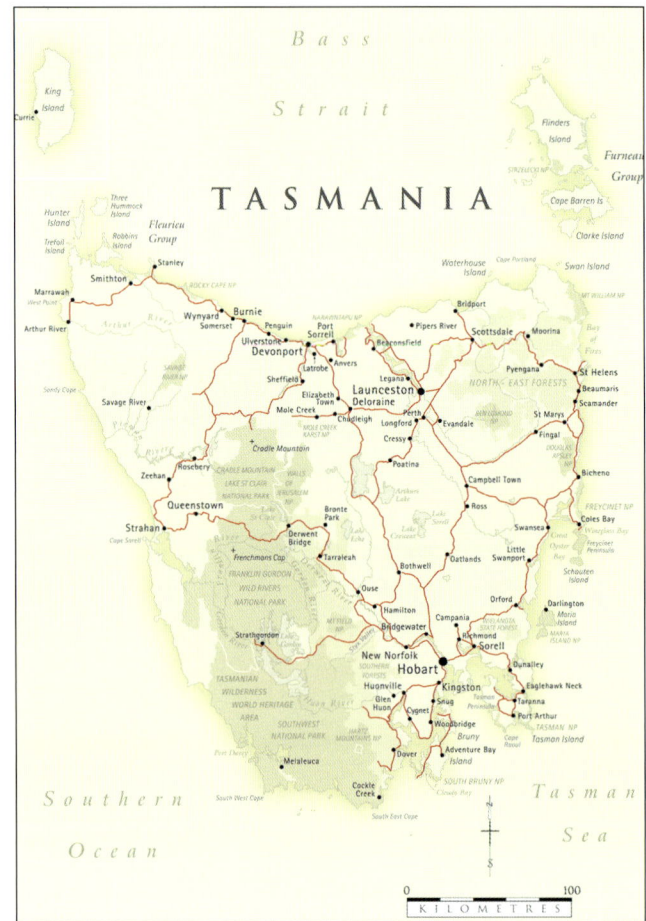

(top left)
Project Bird plumage illustration
Medium Watercolour
Client New Holland Publishers

(top right)
Project Plan for signage
Medium Scenic paint
Client The Wilderness Society

(above left)
Project Editorial illustration
Medium Mixed media
Client Thomsons Publications

(above right)
Project Travel map
Medium Digital
Client Text Pacific

The Mutation Parlour is the design and illustration studio of Jason Atherton. With many years experience as an illustrator, Jason works in both digital and traditional mediums. The Mutation Parlour is all about the creative process of changing, as Jason believes in being as versatile as possible in his work. Jason is a member of Illustrators Australia.

The Mutation Parlour
Jason Atherton

Mobile: 0408 607 083

www.mutationparlour.com
info@mutationparlour.com

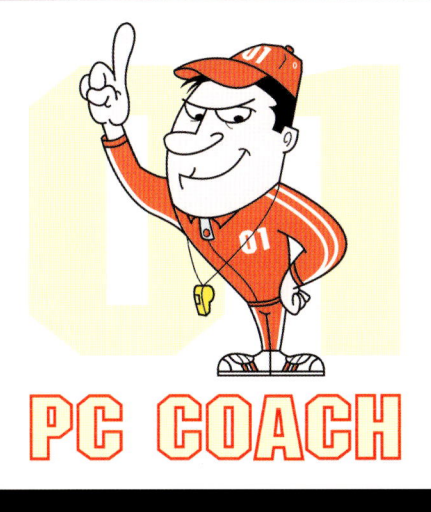

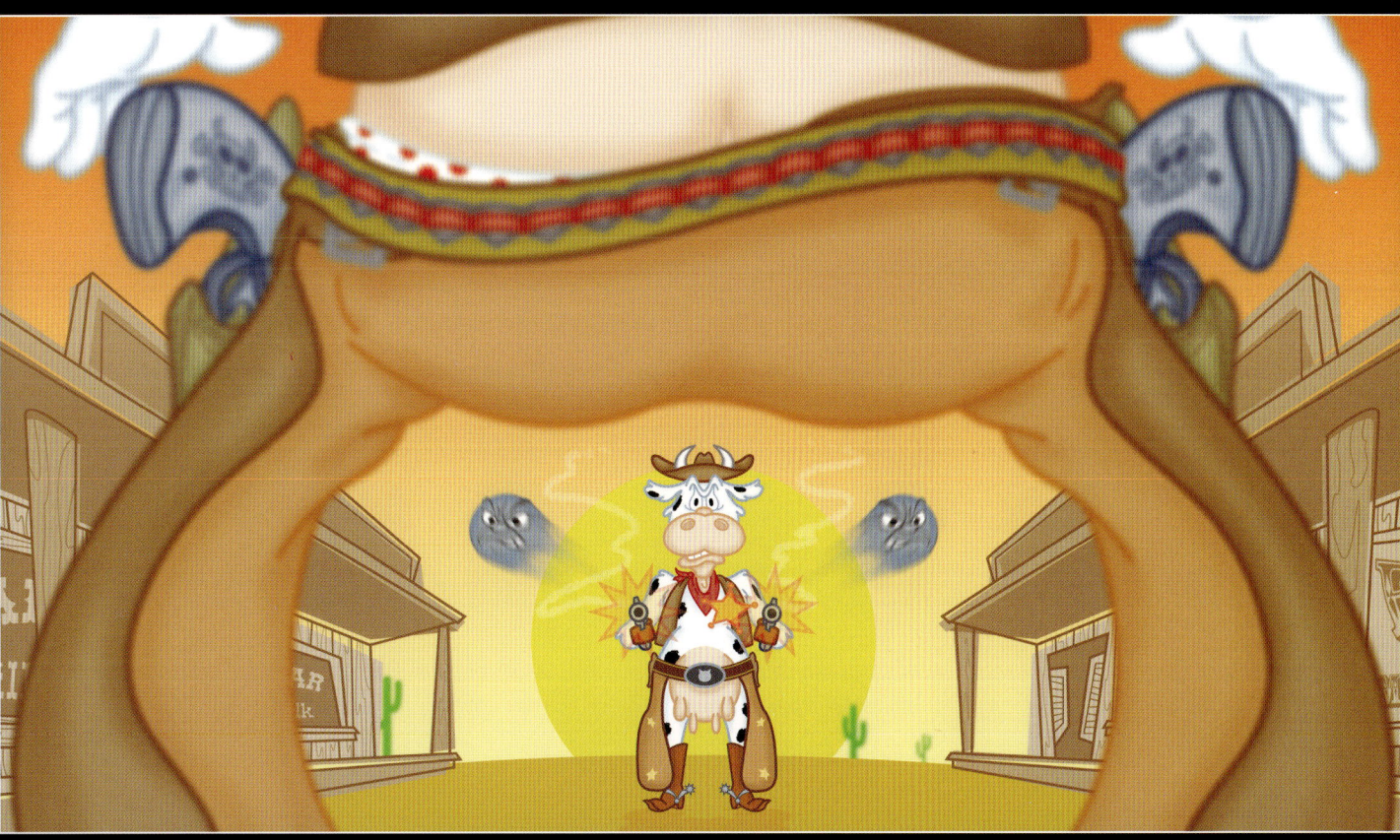

(top left)
Project The PC Coach - logo & identity
Medium Pencil, Adobe Illustrator
Client The PC Coach

(top centre)
Project The Teddy Bears Book Club
Medium Pencil, ink, Corel Painter
Client Promotional illustration

(top right)
Project Pins & Needles with Nurse Cinn - illustration for gothic magazine
Medium Pencil, Adobe Illustrator
Client Fiend

(above)
Project The final showdown with the last carnivore in Moo County
Medium Pencil, Adobe Illustrator, Adobe Photoshop
Client Promotional illustration

Oz Graphix [5] 103

Medical Arts
Dr Levent EFE, CMI

179 Thomas Street
East Brighton VIC 3187

Phone: 0418 356 780
Fax: 03 9578 0978

www.medicalarts.com.au
levent@medicalarts.com.au

Digitally rendered anatomical illustrations with an emphasis on accuracy and impact. We specialise in generating concepts on patient education and pharmaceutical promotion for a broad range of clientele worldwide.

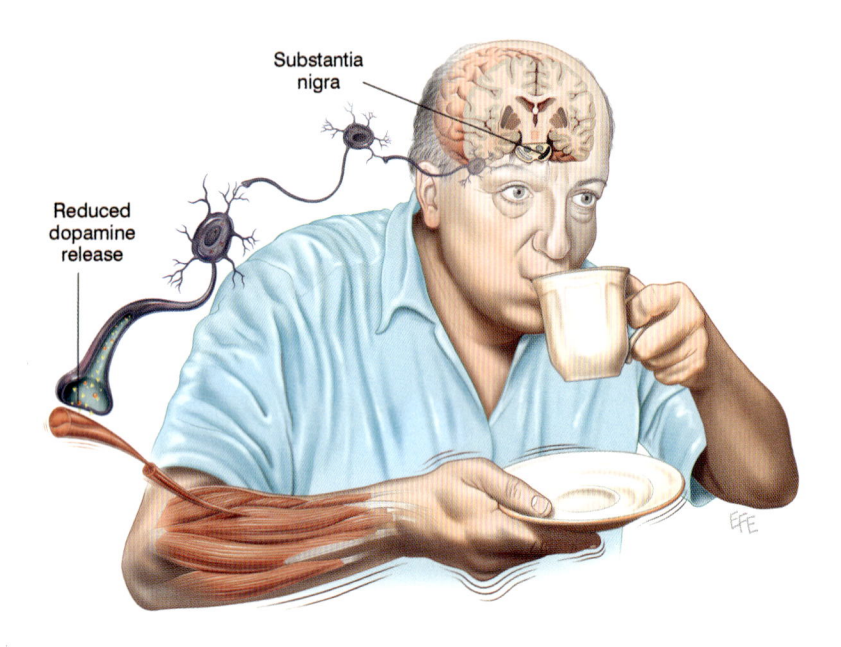

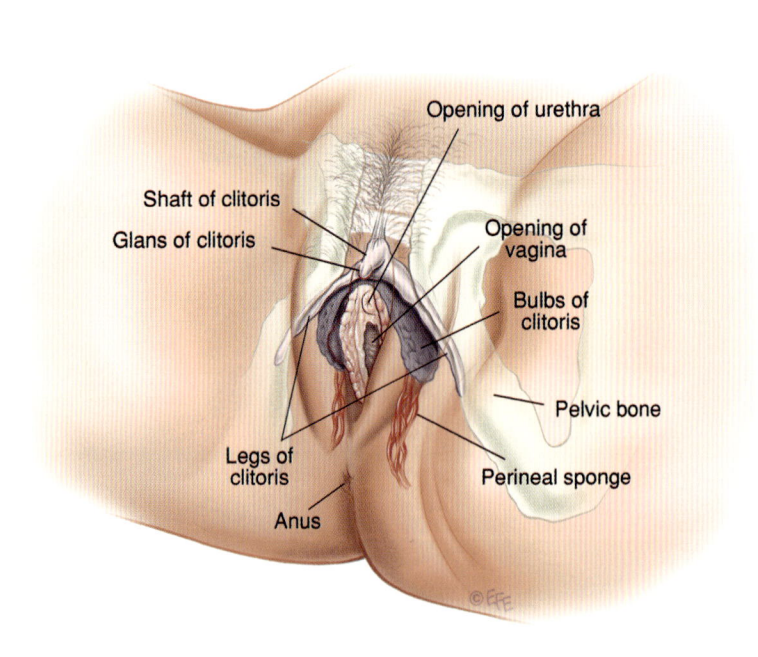

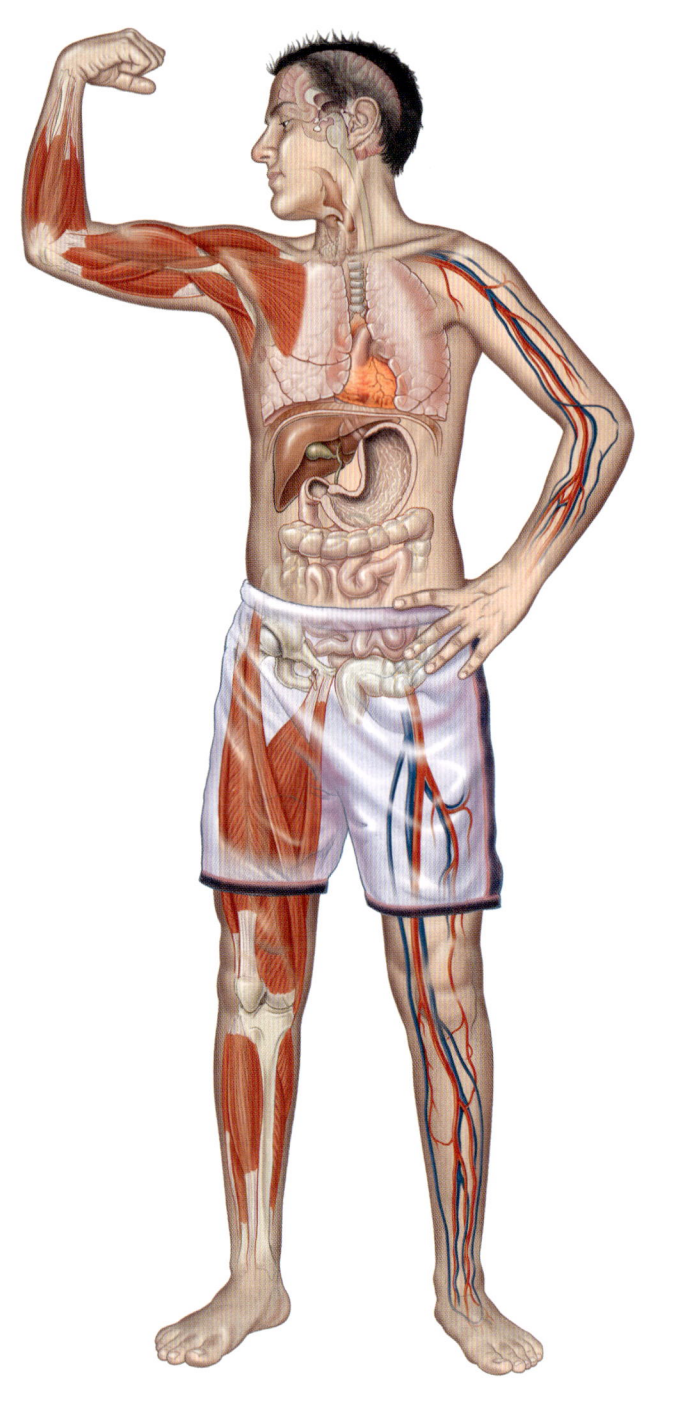

(top left)
Project Parkinson's syndrome
Client Elixir Healthcare Education

(above left)
Project Anatomy of the Clitoris
Client The Elusive Orgasm/ Brightfire Press

(above right)
Project Muscular, digestive and circulatory systems
Client John Wiley & Sons Australia

If there is a mental block just slapping you in the face and you need an imaginative illustration, then drop what you're doing and give Nahum a buzz. Editorial & book illustrations, character designs, animation, storyboards, concept visuals, game visuals and a dab of design—Nahum does it all. Check out what else this zany illustrator has in store at www.nahumziersch.com.au.

NZ Illustration

4 Constance Street
Westbourne Park SA 5041

Phone: 08 8272 5323
Mobile: 0409 671 754
Fax: 08 8339 5556

www.nahumziersch.com.au
nahum_ziersch@chariot.net.au

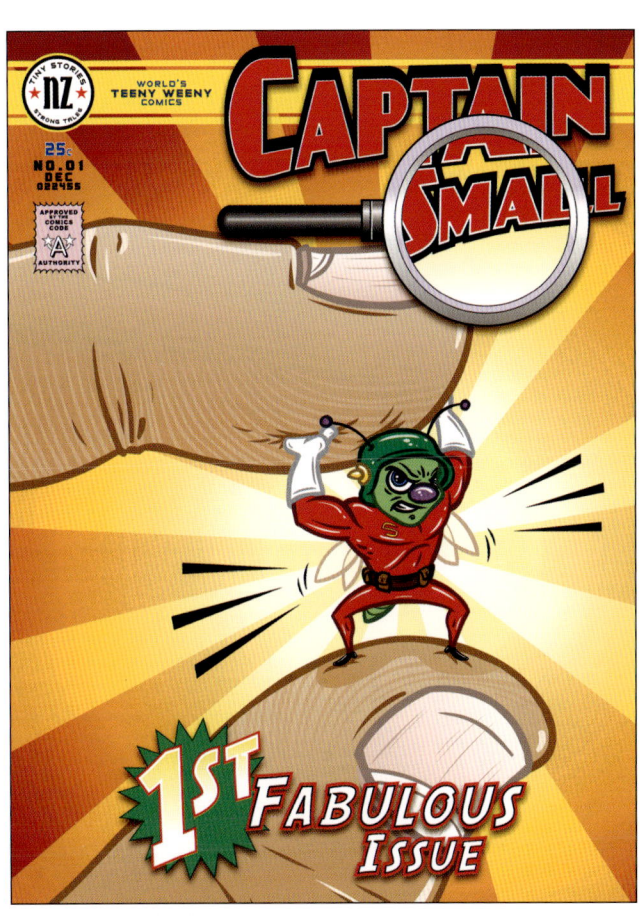

(top left)
Project Captain Small - entered as part of an ad campaign
Client Illustrator's Australia

(top right)
Project Hampster character design/mascot
Client Hampshire Hotel in Adelaide

(above left)
Project Kamanohashi Mountain Warrior character design/mascot
Client NISS - Niseko International Ski School - Japan

(above right)
Project Gnomies - vinyl toy design
Client Self Promotional

Oz Graphix [5]

Squidinc Illustration and Design

PO Box 456
Elwood VIC 3184

Phone: 03 9510 4552
Fax: 03 9525 1960

www.squidinc.com.au
shaun@squidinc.com.au

Shaun Britton has worked as a designer and illustrator for Walt Disney and Warner Bros. Consumer Products for a number of years—in Hong Kong and in Australia. Since starting **Squidinc**, Shaun has worked with many clients, including Twentieth Century Fox, Nike, Coca Cola and Hallmark. His work is a blend of digital and traditional illustration and animation, playful graphic design and quirky character development.

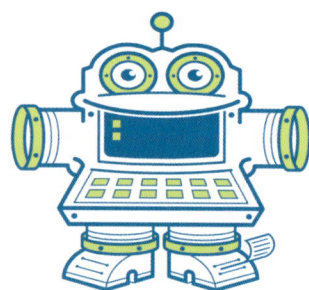

(top)
Project Monster
Client Interactive self promotion piece

(above left, series)
Project Cat and Ladybug
Client Concept illustrations for a Hong Kong greeting card company

(above, centre)
Project ScribbleWalk - Illustration in a Melbourne City-Development pitch document
Client Shannon's Way Advertising

(above right)
Project Computa logo design
Client Paul Franks IT

Susy Boyer has enjoyed life as a freelance illustrator for 19 years. She worked in Brisbane, Sydney and London before settling in her sunny beachside studio on the Gold Coast. A versatile artist, Susy illustrates mainly in hand-rendered watercolour, pencil and pastel, as well as fine art painting in pastel and acrylic on canvas. She works mainly in magazines, children's books and advertising.

Her client list includes:
World Vision,
The Australian Women's Weekly,
House & Garden,
Slimming,
Mother & Baby,
Australian Parents,
Penguin Books,
Pearson Education,
Scholastic,
Macmillan, and
Nelson

Susy Boyer

PO Box 35
Miami QLD 4220

Phone: 07 5554 5394
Mobile: 0413 134 426

www.susyboyer.com
boyerart@bigpond.net.au

(top left)
Project Magazine article 'Vitamin-rich Greens'
Medium Watercolour & coloured pencil
Client Lifestyle Gardens

(top right)
Project Children's book character sketch
Medium Coloured pencil
Client University of WA Press

(above left)
Project Flower painting series
Medium Chalk pastel
Client Personal collection

(above right)
Project Menu illustration
Medium Coloured pencil
Client HQ Hospitality

Oz Graphix [5]

PHOTOGRAPHERS

Doncaster East VIC 3109

Phone: 03 9848 9932
Fax: 03 9848 9968

www.australianscenics.com
images@australianscenics.com

Melbourne professional photographer Peter Walton, Australian Scenics has become the definitive source for Australian landscapes and rural scenes. From their fully searchable website, 1.2Mb JPEGs can be easily previewed and downloaded for use in layouts. Their high resolution scans

publishers and corporations are regular users of their pristine images. Australian Scenics' image categories include: Alpine, Coastal, Lakes & Rivers, Landscapes, Nature, Patterns, Rainforests, Recreation, Roads, Rockscapes, Rural Scenes, Sandscapes, Skies, Treescapes and Waterfalls.

Maynard Imaging represents commercial photographers in Sydney, Brisbane, Perth and Melbourne—providing photography and production services to the advertising, marketing and corporate sectors. Specialising in many varied fields, the photographers work from independent studios equipped with high-end digital and traditional film cameras in all formats. Maynard Imaging manages photography production from small projects to large scale resource-intensive productions. This is made possible though strong affiliations with producers, lifestyle and food stylists, hair & make-up artists, set-builders, prop and wardrobe buyers, caterers and location scouts. Australia-wide, Maynard Imaging photographers share a common purpose: to create imagery that captures the spirit of their clients' products and services.

Maynard Imaging

Level 5, The Works
Creative Industries Precinct
34 Parer Place
Kelvin Grove QLD 4059

Phone: 1300 761 487
07 3337 7902
Fax: 07 3300 0341
www.maynardimaging.com.au
info@maynardimaging.com.au

(top left)
Project Kettle
Photographer Andrew Yeo

(top centre)
Project Stamford Marque
Photographer John Fryz

(top right)
Project Property Solutions
Photographer Shane Holzberger

(above left)
Project Pencils
Photographer Adam Cleave

(above right)
Project ConocoPhillips
Photographer Robert Garvey

Oz Graphix [5] **111**

Momentum Studio

9/31 Thompson Street
Bowen Hills
Brisbane QLD 4006

Phone: 07 3252 4150
Fax: 07 3252 4250

www.momentumstudio.com.au
info@momentumstudio.com.au

Momentum Studio houses a collection of individuals that enjoy and live photography. It is a vibrant, creative environment where business success is due to a great lifestyle, stunning locations and a skilled support team. Momentum Studio provides clients with image capture on high end digital or film equipment, in addition to state of the art photographic and post production facilities. Momentum Studio is a resource centre for knowledge, a hub for production and, importantly, Noosa is only a weekend away.

(top)
Photographer Alex Buckingham
Client Hennessy
Agency Lee Burnetts
Art Director Gordon Hughes

(above left)
Photographer Alan Jensen
Client The Tivoli Theatre

(above right)
Photographer Mark Burgin
Client Calleija Jewellers

Momentum Studio

(top)
Photographer Eric Victor
Client Broncolor Switzerland

(above)
Photographer Andrew Yeo
Client Queensland University of Technology

sam i am photo

Silver Pixel Studios
1/39 Phillip Street
Newtown NSW 2042

Phone: 02 9557 2550
Fax: 02 9557 2559

www.samiam.com.au
sam@samiam.com.au

sam i am photo pride themselves on their artists. Producing a seamless job from concept to delivery is their aim. Representing a small group of artists whose work covers everything from fashion to food, cars to concords, sam i am photo has strengths in each area. A full service production company who enjoy translating the cerebral to the image... realising people's notions.

'Sam i am photo are an inspiring team to work with, resulting in a smooth sailing production on time and on budget.'
—Marcella Sullivan, HOST

'The photography was brilliant, the production superb and my tea had just the right amount of milk in it.'
—Paul Bruce, The Glue Society

(top left)
Project Self commissioned
Hair Samir Samaali

(above left)
Project Self commissioned
Make up MAX

(above right)
Project Artisan for Noise magazine
Photographer Helen White

sam i am photo

(above left)
Project Chef, self commissioned
Photographer Andrew Cowen

(above right)
Project Roger Rogerson for Men's Style Magazine
Photographer Greg Bartley

Oz Graphix [5]

ASSOCIATIONS

Sometimes the truth in something is there without embellishment or fuss.

The Australian Graphic Design Association, AGDA; Australia's largest network of designers, has a broad vision formed by the efforts and care of its membership. The potential of this vision starts by joining. Call 02 9955 3955 or visit agda.com.au for details.

AGDA

BOOK No. 1

BOOK No. 2

BOOK No. 3

BOOK No. 4

BOOK No. 5

BOOK No. 6
Volume 1 & 2

BOOK No. 7
Volume 1 & 2

BOOK No. 8
Volume 1 & 2

BOOK No. 9
Volume 1 & 2

The image-buyers guide to Australian illustration

It's free and out now. Call 1300 720181 or email your contact details to ia@waterfront.net.au for a copy of the IA Source Book No. 9
Illustrators Australia   PO Box 1174, St Kilda South, Victoria 3182

illustrators australia

www.illustratorsaustralia.com

AIPP
Australian Institute of Professional Photography

Supporting Emerging Talent

www.aipp.com.au

Matt Hoyle
2004 Canon Australian
Professional Photographer of the Year

Stand out from the crowd

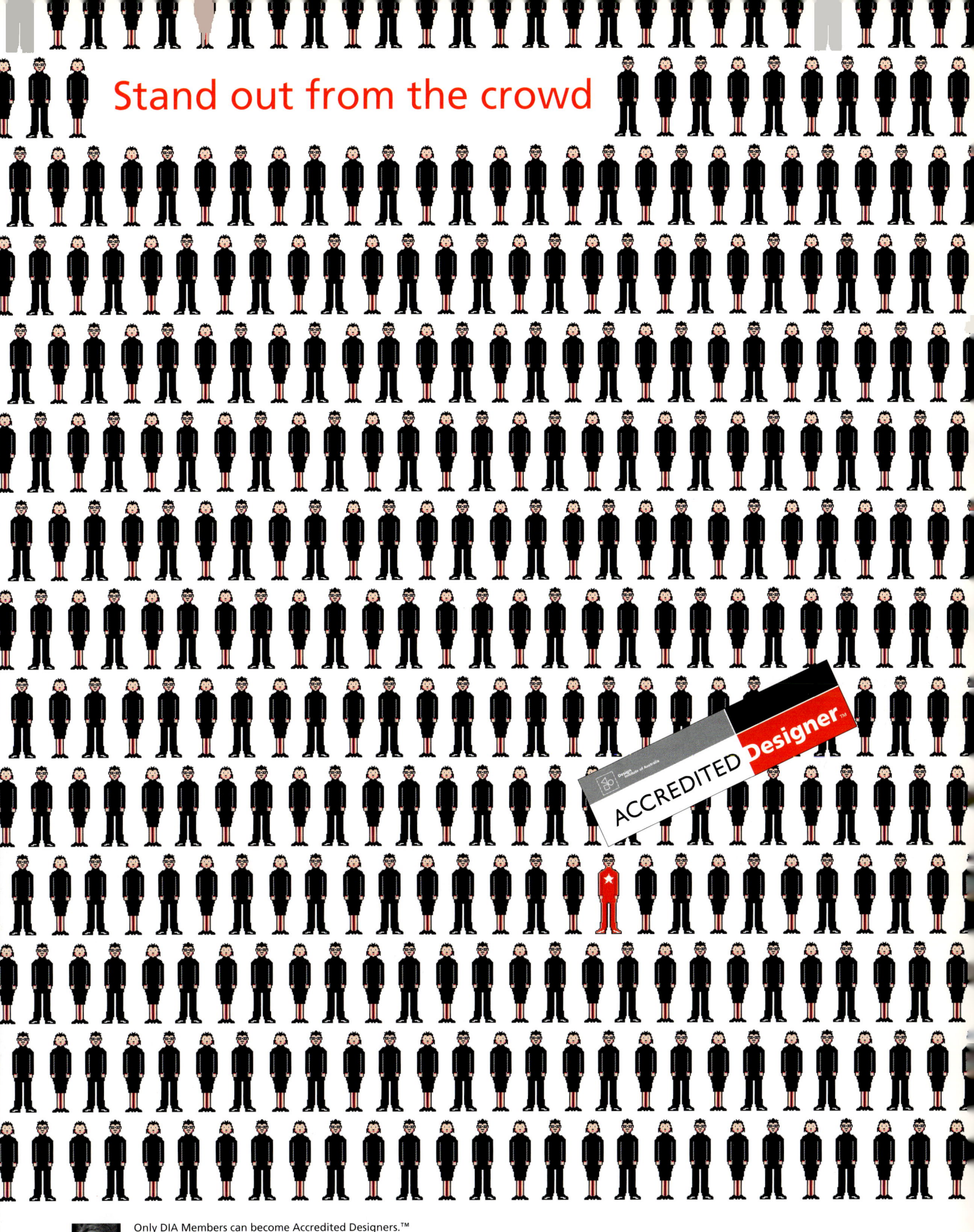

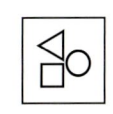

ACCREDITED Designer™

Only DIA Members can become Accredited Designers.™
Join the DIA today – the professional body for all
Australian professional designers.

Contact Phillippa for details and a membership kit.
Tel (03) 8662 5490 admin@design.org.au www.design.org.au

Design Institute of Australia | The Voice of Professional Design

are your digital images behaving themselves?

ACMP

Australia's Commercial
and Media Photographers

Get the ACMP Digital Image
Guidelines for global best
practice image management.
Free at www.acmp.com.au

In today's new world of digital images, choosing the right colourspace and workflow management can make the difference between excellence and disaster. If you don't want to compromise on quality, get the right advice from the people who know their business.

Photograph by Longshots

Oz Graphix [5]

Order form

Please supply .... copies of Oz Graphix [5] as follows:

	currency	rrp	p&p	unit price	Total
Australia (inc. gst)	AUD	$ 24.95	$ 10.00	$ 34.95	....
New Zealand	NZD	$ 29.50	$ 18.00	$ 47.50	....
USA	USD	$ 19.50	$ 10.00	$ 29.50	....
Canada	CND	$ 24.95	$ 10.00	$ 40.00	....
Other countries	AUD	$ 20.00	$ 18.00	$ 38.00	....

Credit cards will be charged at the current exchange rate and billed in local currencies.

Name ....

Company/School ....

Address ....

City/Suburb/Postcode ....

Country ....

Phone ....

Email ....

Payment is by: ☐ Cheque made payable to Design Graphics

☐ Bankcard   ☐ VISA   ☐ Mastercard   ☐ American Express

Name on credit card ....

Credit card number ....

Expiry date ....

Signature ....

Mail
Design Graphics
PO Box 10
Ferny Creek VIC 3786
Australia

Fax
Australian orders: 03 9755 1155
International orders: +61 3 9755 1155

2005

☐ Yes, I would like to be added to your mailing list.

Email ....

Oz Graphix [5]

INDEX

Afterimage Graphic Design and Photography

21 Budd Street
Collingwood VIC 3066

Phone: 03 9416 3689
Fax: 03 9416 2998
www.afterimage.com.au
admin@afterimage.com.au

.........................p14

Afterimage pride themselves on their mutually beneficial partnership with clients, offering a wealth of information and support in design, advertising, marketing and related areas. Established in 1990, Afterimage values its reputation in producing exceptional work across a range of industries.
The talented and innovative team possess a wide variety of skills and expertise in design and advertising. They provide a complete service from concept to implementation and delivery for catalogues, brochures, advertising, corporate identity, digital photography and web design. Afterimage reflects the true nature of their clients' business by developing an in-depth understanding of their products and services. They offer personalised attention, including ongoing consultation and follow-up at every stage of production.

AG Design

Phone: 0405 432866
www.agdesign.net.au
anna@agdesign.net.au

.........................p15

Anna Godwin, Sydney based designer and illustrator, creates mostly digital imagery for the publishing, advertising and design industries. A background in design enables her to understand and take a productive role in the creative process, producing pencil roughs and visualising ideas at concept stage. Although her style lends itself to children's illustration and character development, Anna receives a wide variety of commissions from clients locally and overseas.

APR Design

96-98 Bluff Road
Black Rock VIC 3193

Phone: 03 9598 3588
Fax: 03 9597 0630
www.aprdesign.com.au
info@aprdesign.com.au

.........................p16

APR Design are design specialists providing packaging solutions and below-the-line advertising support to high profile FMCG companies.
Our dedicated team works closely with marketing and sales professionals to build a solid strategic approach, coupled with exceptional creative to ensure success for every project.

Australian Scenics

Suite 10A
857 Doncaster Road
Doncaster East VIC 3109

Phone: 03 9848 9932
Fax: 03 9848 9968
www.australianscenics.com
images@australianscenics.com

.........................p110

Australian Scenics is a highly focused digital stock library born out of a passion for the Australian landscape. Established in 1995 by Melbourne professional photographer Peter Walton, Australian Scenics has become the definitive source for Australian landscapes and rural scenes. From their fully searchable website, 1.2Mb JPEGs can be easily previewed and downloaded for use in layouts. Their high resolution scans have been expertly prepared for quality print reproduction.
Major Australian advertising agencies, graphic designers, publishers and corporations are regular users of their pristine images.
Australian Scenics' image categories include: Alpine, Coastal, Lakes & Rivers, Landscapes, Nature, Patterns, Rainforests, Recreation, Roads, Rockscapes, Rural Scenes, Sandscapes, Skies, Treescapes and Waterfalls.

Balance Design Group

PO Box 1425
Neutral Bay NSW 2089

Phone: 02 9922 1099
Fax: 02 8920 1768
www.balance.com.au
stuart@balance.com.au

.........................p18

We were born to design!
Balance Design Group is a Sydney based agency specialising in corporate branding, dynamic website design and systems development. With over twenty years in business, and nine years digital experience, behind us, clients can be assured of high quality creative combined with smooth project implementation.
Our experience and history has made Balance Design one of the most effective and well respected digital agencies in Sydney.

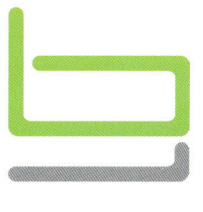

Bastian Group p20

4 Ross Place
South Melbourne VIC 3004

Phone: 03 8676 7504
Fax: 03 8676 7505
www.bastiangroup.com.au
info@bastiangroup.com.au

Bastian Group understands that the changing face of business has produced a more openly competitive operating environment. We have no illusions that the challenge is to find smarter ways of developing new communication models and practices that will advance our clients' competitive market positioning. This we believe can only be achieved through cutting-edge thinking that truly cuts it with an audience. Our complete range of services range from advertising, marketing and branding to design, packaging and corporate identity services. Our range of services are centralised around our strategic way of thinking—we are not afraid to ask the question, why?

Bill Wood Illustration p94

24 Goold Street
Burwood VIC 3125

Phone: 03 9888 0011
Fax: 03 9833 4577
www.illustration.com.au
billwood@illustration.com.au

Is communication important to you? Bill Wood Illustration has been in the business of communication in Australia and overseas since 1988. With a small but dedicated team of three, we employ a wide range of styles and techniques to suit a variety of projects. Our diverse range of clients hail from the fields of advertising, design, packaging, direct marketing and publishing. Keeping a low profile when promoting our work, Bill Wood Illustration prefers the reliable, but tested positive word-of-mouth approach, allowing us to maintain a loyal regular customer base.

Black Squid Design p17

203 Melbourne Street
North Adelaide SA 5006

Phone: 08 8361 8066
www.blacksquid.com.au
info@blacksquid.com.au

Design based around ideas generation and visual communication, to do the unexpected, accept risk and emphasise what is new, maintaining identity and appeal. Design intellectually driven solutions that best answer the clients' brief. To explore all avenues remembering the element of surprise. But most importantly – have fun.

Blue Marlin Brand Design p22

Melbourne
7 Meaden Street
Southbank VIC 3006
Phone: 03 9694 5900
Fax: 03 9694 5999

Sydney
Level 3, 5 Queen Street
Chippendale NSW 2008
Phone: 02 9698 3277
Fax: 02 9698 2677
www.bluemarlinbd.com
ozcrew1@bluemarlinbd.com.au

Blue Marlin is a strategically focused brand design agency that delivers outstanding identity, graphic and structural packaging design for many of Australia's key FMCG and retail companies.
By focusing on complete consumer & brand environment understanding, we produce creative solutions that achieve considerable cut-through for our clients' brands.
This approach is applied to visual and corporate identity as well as product innovation, NPD and in-depth brand strategy.
Highlighted here is a snapshot of our Australian work, all of which achieved or exceeded our clients' marketing objectives through comprehensive and effective brand design solutions.
While we continuously focus on each market's independent nuances, our global resources in Australia, the UK, Europe, Asia and America allow us to learn from, and have an influence on, global design trends.
Just like the many powerful brands we work with, we can't stand still.

Brave Communications p26

Level 3, 55 Chandos Street
St Leonards NSW 2065

Phone: 02 9439 2344
Fax: 02 9439 4537
www.bravecomm.com.au
studio@bravecomm.com.au

Brave Communications is a strategic design consultancy offering a comprehensive range of services; brand strategy, packaging (graphics & form), corporate communications and brand activation—thus delivering an integrated experience across all areas of visual communication.
We believe that strong brands are built on a shared vision of the future; on true customer and market understanding. Together with our clients, we create solutions that are brave, dynamic and innovative.
In a Brave future, the businesses that will grow and make a difference are those that embrace change, and are willing to acquire the new skills and capabilities needed to do so.

Cowan

Melbourne
220 High Street
Prahran VIC 3181
Phone: 03 9521 2422
Fax: 03 9521 2929

Sydney
239 Pacific Highway
North Sydney NSW 2060
Phone: 02 9929 9177
Fax: 02 9929 3672
www.cowandesign.com

...........................p28

Creating: At Cowan, we understand the importance of achieving a balance between the emotional and rational cues within brand campaigns. Such balance is crucial if brand values and product benefits are to be communicated successfully. Through creativity, essential information can be delivered in a memorable way to demand the desired response from the target audience.

Brand: A brand is more than a logo. It is a powerful visual language that communicates with the consumer and creates a lasting bond. Fundamental to our philosophy is the understanding of the relationship that can be developed between the brand and the consumer. Our process forges links and delivers clear messages to the market, without relying on words alone.

Campaigns: The prosperity of a brand is not dependent on any individual piece of communication, but a multifaceted program of events delivered over time. In any brand project, our design strategies are based upon the bigger picture. This provides a platform for campaigns that are carefully constructed, specifically targeted and cleverly executed.

D MAX

1 Pinewood Drive
Mount Waverley VIC 3149

Phone: 03 9803 5804
Fax: 03 9803 5814
www.dmaxpl.com.au
chris@dmaxpl.com.au

...........................p96

D MAX has produced an extensive range of illustrations for a variety of clients in the design, advertising and publishing industries. All of these illustrations have been produced using a combination of LightWave and Photoshop. Chris Hughes established D MAX over ten years ago and provides a range of design, advertising, illustration, 3D, website design, CD Rom and television/video services.
Design to the MAX!

David Trewern Design (DTDesign)

Melbourne
117 Green Street
Richmond VIC 3121
Phone: 03 9429 2799
Fax: 03 9429 8706

Sydney (STW Group)
Level 45, Citigroup Centre
2 Park Street
Sydney NSW 2000
Phone: 02 9268 1735
www.dtdesign.com
info@dtdesign.com

...........................p30

David Trewern Design (DTDesign) is a specialist internet development studio, focusing on creatively-driven internet strategy, design and technology. Founded in 1996, it is one of Australia's most innovative, experienced and awarded web development firms.

Deborah Niland

Phone: 02 9460 7442
Fax: 02 9460 7443
www.deborah-niland.com.au
d.niland@bigpond.net.au

...........................p97

Deborah Niland is a freelance artist and illustrator. She has a special interest in children's books and has a list of successful titles to her name. In addition she has illustrated for a variety of publications, newspapers and magazines. In her work, Deborah employs different styles—traditional and digital. She particularly enjoys illustrating stories that are humorous and character based, with pigs and hippos being definite favourites!

Dee Texidor - Illustrator and Designer

'Narraburra'
1907 Deer Vale Road
Deer Vale NSW 2453

Phone: 02 6657 3355
Mobile: 0417 859 105
deetexidor.com
dee@texidor.com

...........................p98

Dee Texidor has worked in Graphic design and illustration for 17 years in marketing and publishing. Following two years as an inhouse designer and illustrator for Scholastic Australia, Dee began her foray into freelance illustration.
Dee's first children's picture/novelty book 'Tiny Turtles' (2001) for The Book Company has gone into reprint several times, and she has created over 30 books since.
Clients include Dolly, Total Girl, For Me, Women's Weekly magazine, New Frontier, Scholastic, Blake Education, Thomson Learning, Ice Water Press and Children's Book Council. She enjoys working in bright watercolours, pastels and digital illustration.

DeMo Design p32

373 Riley Street
Surry Hills NSW 2010

Phone: 02 9211 2966
Fax: 02 9211 2969
www.demodesign.com.au
mail@demodesign.com.au

DeMo are specialists in packaging design for FMCG. Our personable, creative team focuses on outstanding and innovative solutions, because innovation lies at the heart of both better design and better business.
Through dialogue with our clients, we bridge the gap between brand strategy and brand execution, communicating core values to make a positive connection with the consumer. Our design expertise includes; new product development, brand updates, structural packaging and research stimulus.

Design Itch p38

1a Chapman Street
Charlestown NSW 2290

Phone: 02 4943 6623
Fax: 02 4943 6624
www.designitch.com.au
hello@designitch.com.au

Design Itch is always ready for creative challenges and new itches to scratch.
Since 1999, Design Itch has been creating fresh design solutions to help a variety of organisations achieve their unique goals. They have eagerly invested much time developing a specialised design process to ensure seamless project management, and they believe that good relationships and open communication form the basis of successful design.
Design Itch insists on creating results-orientated solutions that deliver a positive image of confidence, professionalism and individuality.

---

designCentric p34

163 Gilles Street
Adelaide SA 5000

Phone: 08 8232 3377
Fax: 08 8232 3766
www.designcentric.com.au
ask@designcentric.com.au

designCentric continues to be chosen by clients who value innovation, creativity and functionality in design. With an excellent record of project management, designCentric offers the complete range of graphic design, brand development and strategic communications.

Disegno Group p36

129 Queensbridge Street
Southbank VIC 3006

Phone: 03 9690 0905
Fax: 03 9690 0906
www.disegno.com.au
enquiry@disegno.com.au

Disegno brings corporate and brand management, strategic marketing and creative visual thinking together to solve clients' marketing challenges. Combining extensive experience in Australia and overseas with a young, committed team, the group can handle projects of all sizes, from corporate design to product packaging to in-house internet project design and implementation.
A loyal clientele and successful track record prove the effectiveness and value of Disegno's integrated approach.

Double Happy p99

1/19 Lyndhurst Crescent
Hawthorn VIC 3122

Phone: 03 9819 0586
Mobile: 0400 188 170
www.doublehappy.net
info@doublehappy.net

Type doublehappy.net into your web browser and you half expect an Adults Only warning and a barrage of 'Barely Legal' pop-ups. Instead, you arrive safe and warm in illustrator, Dane Flighty's world of unique characters and flash animations. Dane's illustrations have appeared in IDN and Australian Financial Review's 'Boss' magazine—to name a few.

Emma Broe

Lot 80, Castle Street
Kirup WA 6251

Phone: 08 9731 6450
Fax: 08 9731 6450
www.emmabroe.com
emmabroe@wn.com.au

............................p39

Emma Broe has over 13 years experience in all aspects of graphic design and web development from concepts to application, in areas ranging from packaging, point of sale and corporate literature through to international magazine design and advertising. Clients include: Ford UK, Nissan GB, Henkel, Department of Education & Training, WA and businesses based both Australia wide and overseas.

Genie Creative

Level 2, 21 Oxford Street
Darlinghurst NSW 2010

Phone: 02 9283 4700
www.geniecreative.com.au
info@geniecreative.com.au

............................p40

Genie Creative are specialists in web design and development, flash animation and online advertising.
They excel in creating a diverse selection of online solutions that mixes outstanding creativity with intuitive functionality. They have produced work for AGL, LJ Hooker, RACQ, Select Appointments, Unoduo and Vodafone—to name a few.

Girling Design

Suite 108,
89 High Street
Kew VIC 3101

Phone: 03 9854 6166
Mobile: 0418 505 241
www.girlingdesign.com.au
nick@girlingdesign.com.au

............................p41

During a lunch break, Nick's four year old cousin said that Girling Design was the best graphic design business in the universe and that he wanted to work there. Nick replied, 'Thanks mate, with that kind of optimism I want you to be my Client Liaison Manager.' He smiled and replied, 'Do I get to draw pictures with you?'
Girling Design is a specialist graphic and web design firm, striving to produce well formed and effective branding. Nicholas Girling is the creative director, having over ten years design experience.

---

house mouse design

Level 2, 4-10 Bank Place
Melbourne VIC 3000

Phone: 03 9602 5855
Fax: 03 9602 4252
www.housemouse.com.au
mail@housemouse.com.au

............................p42

house mouse design is a graphic design firm, centrally located in Melbourne's CBD, and has been established since 1996.
The firm employs a team of graphic designers, all sharing the common goal—to communicate effectively and successfully through graphic design.
house mouse design provides a graphic communication service to a range of clients whose output includes annual reports, publications, promotional material, packaging, branding and brochures; and has the resources to steer all projects from original concept to final product.

HSJ Design Group

1056 Dandenong Road
Carnegie VIC 3163

Phone: 03 9571 6158
Fax: 03 9571 3993
www.hsj.com.au
ian@hsj.com.au

............................p43

The HSJ Design Group was formed in 1975 and retains the same management today. The group offers copywriting, art direction, design, print management, digital photography, television and radio production, web design and account service.
The group's speciality is photography based catalogues for both trade and consumer, with clients as diverse as mining giant, Rio Tinto, through to retail giant, Nike.

Ian F Faulkner and Associates p102

44 Riverview Road
Clareville NSW 2107

Phone: 02 9973 1928
Fax: 02 9973 3221
www.ianfaulknerillustrator.com
iffaulk@ozemail.com.au

As an illustrator, cartographer and cartoonist, I am always trying to present information in as informative and interesting manner as possible. Please visit my website for more varied samples of my work.

Icon Partners p44

Level 3, 448 St Kilda Road
Melbourne VIC 3004

Phone: 03 9867 4890
Fax: 03 9867 5890
www.iconpartners.com.au
info@iconpartners.com.au

Icon Partners is a multi disciplined design company with a broad skill base incorporating brand identity, packaging, environmental graphics and print communication. We deliver an integrated approach from research and concept through to product design and market communication.
We provide clients with the highest level of quality service by maximising the brand's potential and strategically integrating all levels of visual communication to promote a unified and sound message in the market place.
The incorporation of Icon Raremedia into our business model enables us to offer a truly 'through the line' seamless solution with digital media design and applications.

Icon Raremedia p46

Level 1, 214 Graham Street
Port Melbourne VIC 3207

Phone: 03 9646 2544
www.rare.com.au
info@rare.com.au

With a core focus in design, Icon Raremedia specialises in the creation of electronic media that communicates and compels. We develop customised, effective and innovative solutions to complex communication situations. Our skills cover the breadth of digital media design and production including internet sites, games, CD-Rom development, multimedia sales presentations and touchscreen kiosks. We have experience with a broad range of clients from global corporations and government agencies to educational institutions, catering to their specific and very individual needs.

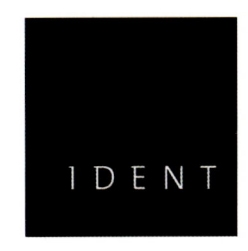

Ident p48

Suite 9, Jones Bay Wharf
26-32 Pirrama Road
Pyrmont NSW 2009

Phone: 02 9571 1400
Fax: 02 9571 1250
www.identbrand.com
studio@identbrand.com

Ident is a team of branding specialists who are inspired by creative excellence and motivated by your objectives. An award winning design consultancy, Ident specialise in branding, corporate identities and packaging. To every project we bring the eyes of enthusiastic consumers and the strategic minds of branding experts.

Image & Substance p50

Suite 3, 26 The Parade West
Kent Town SA 5067

Phone: 08 8363 9655
Fax: 08 8363 2120
www.imageandsubstance.com.au
clients@imageandsubstance.com.au

Established in 1995, Image & Substance offers specific expertise in both graphic design and website design/construction. The name of our company is symbolic of our determination to provide design services (Image) that clearly reflect an understanding of your business (Substance). We do not just draw pretty pictures!
Image & Substance has a team of young designers who offer a fresh approach to the simple, effective design of logos and stationery, annual reports and corporate publications, exhibition displays, signage, websites and digital design.

Interbrand Australia p52

Level 2, 174 Queen Street
Melbourne VIC 3000

Phone: 03 9670 5333
Fax: 03 9670 4200
www.interbrand.com.au
contact@interbrand.com.au

Interbrand manages, creates and values brands. Interbrand is known worldwide as the leading source of intellectual property, information and thought leadership on all facets of branding. Across 26 offices, Interbrand employs people with a diverse range of experiences—all united by their belief in the positive and meaningful influence that brands can have in society. Interbrand works across a multitude of disciplines including design—brand identities, signage; and packaging—naming, brand strategy and brand valuation.

---

ism Graphic Design p54

5 Ballarat Street
Brunswick VIC 3056

Phone: 03 9387 7677
Fax: 03 9387 7877
www.ismgraphicdesign.com.au
ism@ismgraphicdesign.com.au

ism Graphic Design is an enthusiastic and passionate consultancy studio with a strong focus on brand development, management and implementation. We make sure our clients receive maximum benefit and market coverage. This is achieved through understanding client marketing objectives and the target audience.
Driven to achieve long-term results, it is not only the destination we find important for our clients, but also the journey.

James Hart Design p100

PO Box 817
Mornington VIC 3931

Mobile: 0403 722 211
www.jameshart.com.au
info@jameshart.com.au

James Hart Design is an illustration and design studio based on the Mornington Peninsula, near Melbourne. James Hart is a digital and traditional illustrator focused on providing creative solutions for companies seeking identification, advertising, graphic art, concept development, character design and visualisation across all media. James was raise on animated TV shows of the 80s, video games and comics. His passion for character design and the human condition has helped him produce illustrations for clients including: John Wiley & Sons, UC Publishing and Mercury Mobility.

Joseph Casni Design Management p56

20 Stalwart Street
Prairiewood NSW 2176

Phone: 02 9756 0750
Fax: 02 9604 0160
oneeyedesign@lycos.com

'Creating a viable branded reality that explores and satisfies both the client needs and openly allows for creative visual experimentation are the two fundamental keys needed for effective brand managing.'
Joseph's simple, yet effective philosophy about the exploration of suitable branded identity and management creates a language of style and perception that visually speaks directly to its desired audience.

Latitude Group p58

7 Phoenix Street
South Yarra VIC 3141

Phone: 03 9826 6199
Fax: 03 9824 2581
www.latitudegroup.com.au
info@latitudegroup.com.au

Latitude is a young creative agency quickly establishing a reputation as a genuine alternative to the major studios with an unmatched combination of services, strategy and fresh thinking. Since appearing on the radar, Latitude has worked on a variety of projects for many businesses from finance to fashion. This way we haven't developed formulae or clichéd ideas about how your project should look or work. Each new client brings a new business approach that demands a new communication approach, which is why we begin with a strategy rather than a favourite colour. At Latitude we share an ambition beyond getting the job done, and believe the true measure of our success rests in the performance of our finished products and the continued satisfaction of our clients. We provide a comprehensive creative service including: all aspects of design, branding, advertising, web, new media, photography and environmental design.

Liveworm Studio

226 Grey Street
South Bank QLD 4101

Phone: 07 3875 6191
Fax: 07 3875 6194
www.liveworm.com.au
design@liveworm.com.au

...........................p60

Liveworm is the professional graphic design studio of the Queensland College of Art, Griffith University. The studio unleashes the creative and commercial potential of the college's undergraduate and postgraduate students of design. Successful projects have been completed for clients within the public sector and private enterprise. Liveworm is making design come alive for students and clients alike.

Maynard Imaging

Level 5, The Works
Creative Industries Precinct
34 Parer Place
Kelvin Grove QLD 4059

Phone: 1300 761 487
07 3337 7902
Fax: 07 3300 0341
www.maynardimaging.com.au
info@maynardimaging.com.au

...........................p111

Maynard Imaging represents commercial photographers in Sydney, Brisbane, Perth and Melbourne—providing photography and production services to the advertising, marketing and corporate sectors. Specialising in many varied fields, the photographers work from independent studios equipped with high-end digital and traditional film cameras in all formats.
Maynard Imaging manages photography production from small projects to large scale resource-intensive productions. This is made possible though strong affiliations with producers, lifestyle and food stylists, hair & make-up artists, set-builders, prop and wardrobe buyers, caterers and location scouts.
Australia-wide, Maynard Imaging photographers share a common purpose: to create imagery that captures the spirit of their clients' products and services.

MDM Design Associates

Melbourne
25 William Street
Richmond VIC 3121
Phone: 03 9429 1177
Fax: 03 9429 9977

Sydney
Level 2, 50 York Street
Sydney NSW 2000
Phone: 1300 761 108
Fax: 02 8243 1122
www.mdmdesign.com.au
mdm@mdmdesign.com.au

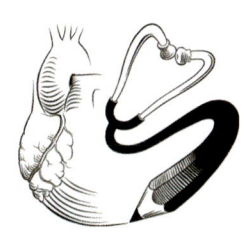

...........................p62

MDM Design is a corporate communications firm established over 13 years ago. The company specialises in branding and identity, and in producing investor communication.

Medical Arts
Dr Levent EFE, CMI

179 Thomas Street
East Brighton VIC 3187

Phone: 0418 356 780
Fax: 03 9578 0978
www.medicalarts.com.au
levent@medicalarts.com.au

...........................p104

Digitally rendered anatomical illustrations with an emphasis on accuracy and impact. We specialise in generating concepts on patient education and pharmaceutical promotion for a broad range of clientele worldwide.

Mekanica

268 Victoria Road
Thornbury VIC 3071

Phone: 03 9484 3578
Fax: 03 9758 4767
www.mekanica.com.au
info@mekanica.com.au

...........................p61

Mekanica is a media design business that is grounded in resolving clients' needs with strong creative conceptualisation across the areas of broadcast, interactive, print and exhibition design. The studio focuses on providing challenging design, motion graphics and animation solutions that seamlessly implement brand strategies across all media.

Momentum Studio p113

9/31 Thompson Street
Bowen Hills
Brisbane QLD 4006

Phone: 07 3252 4150
Fax: 07 3252 4250
www.momentumstudio.com.au
info@momentumstudio.com.au

Momentum Studio houses a collection of individuals that enjoy and live photography. It is a vibrant, creative environment where business success is due to a great lifestyle, stunning locations and a skilled support team.
Momentum Studio provides clients with image capture on high end digital or film equipment, in addition to state of the art photographic and post production facilities. Momentum Studio is a resource centre for knowledge, a hub for production and, importantly, Noosa is only a weekend away.

Monitor Graphics p66

Level 1/1A Yarra Street
South Yarra VIC 3141

Phone: 03 9826 8744
Fax: 03 9826 8544
www.monitorgraphics.com.au
design@monitorgraphics.com.au

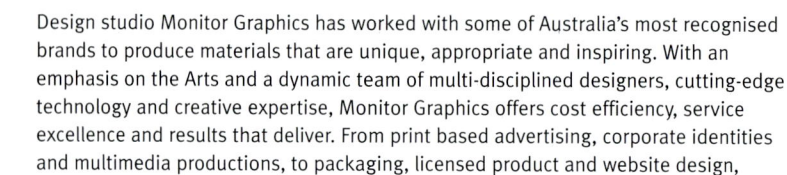

Design studio Monitor Graphics has worked with some of Australia's most recognised brands to produce materials that are unique, appropriate and inspiring. With an emphasis on the Arts and a dynamic team of multi-disciplined designers, cutting-edge technology and creative expertise, Monitor Graphics offers cost efficiency, service excellence and results that deliver. From print based advertising, corporate identities and multimedia productions, to packaging, licensed product and website design, Monitor Graphics offers complete end-to-end design and marketing solutions.

Moon Design p64

38 Boronia Street
Redfern East NSW 2016

Phone: 02 9690 2999
Fax: 02 9698 0576
www.moondesign.com.au
mail@moondesign.com.au

Moon is a Sydney-based strategic branding, communications and design agency with an international reputation for excellence. Creative as well as effective, the agency continues to set new standards through campaigns that fuse together the traditional disciplines of design, advertising and branding—with proven results.
This award-winning agency has built an enviable reputation through a wide and varied client list including Qantas, Sydney Symphony, Sydney Theatre Company, Hutchison 3, Orange, Seafolly, Trent Nathan, Van Heusen, Jetstar and Nike.

The Mutation Parlour
Jason Atherton p103

Mobile: 0408 607 083
www.mutationparlour.com
info@mutationparlour.com

The Mutation Parlour is the design and illustration studio of Jason Atherton. With many years experience as an illustrator, Jason works in both digital and traditional mediums. The Mutation Parlour is all about the creative process of changing, as Jason believes in being as versatile as possible in his work. Jason is a member of Illustrators Australia.

NZ Illustration p105

4 Constance Street
Westbourne Park SA 5041

Phone: 08 8272 5323
Mobile: 0409 671 754
Fax: 08 8339 5556
www.nahumziersch.com.au
nahum_ziersch@chariot.net.au

If there is a mental block just slapping you in the face and you need an imaginative illustration, then drop what you're doing and give Nahum a buzz. Editorial & book illustrations, character designs, animation, storyboards, concept visuals, game visuals and a dab of design—Nahum does it all. Check out what else this zany illustrator has in store at www.nahumziersch.com.au.

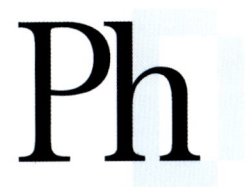

PhD

52 Ourimbah Road
Mosman NSW 2088

Phone: 02 9968 4022
Fax: 02 9968 4822
www.phdcreative.net
studio@pacifichighway.net

.........................p68

PhD provides strategic planning and design solutions to corporate and marketing management.
Our focus is to develop powerful expressions for your brand and create business value and growth.
- Strategic planning
- Corporate & brand development
- Packaging
- Retail visual communications
- Print communications
- Web design & development

Percept Creative Group

PO Box 189
Cronulla NSW 2230

Phone: 02 9544 3200
Fax: 02 9544 5600
www.percept.com.au
lewis@percept.com.au

.........................p67

Percept Creative Group aim to listen, understand and improve the public perception of the businesses they work with. This is done by exciting themselves and their clients about a brand's personality, and then developing design solutions that trigger the desired market response. Their goal is to enjoy all client relationships—delivering service and product that ensure the experience is positive—and to share in the delight of each project's outcome and its benefit to that business.

Plutonium

Level 1, 332-342 Lorimer Street
Port Melbourne VIC 3207

Phone: 03 9684 1247
Fax: 03 9684 1206
www.dpa.com.au
peter@dpa.com.au
stuart@dpa.com.au

.........................p70

Plutonium is a Melbourne based design agency dedicated to providing effective creative solutions. They have a strong focus on generating dynamic communication, an open working environment and strong client relationships.
Armed with a team of multi-disciplined designers, state of the art technology and creative expertise, Plutonium promotes and nurtures a creative language and intelligence rarely found in today's design society.

Rokat Design

Suite A, Level 1
520 Dorset Road
Croydon South VIC 3136

Phone: 03 9725 7316
Fax: 03 9725 2114
www.rokatdesign.com.au
info@rokatdesign.com.au

.........................p72

Understanding that design plays an integral part in the image of all businesses, Rokat Design is committed to creating unique, original and innovative solutions to any visual communication challenge. Rokat will take you on a smooth ride from research, brainstorming and initial concept designs through to printing, production or web publishing, ensuring that you are kept informed and in control throughout the entire trip. Great design fuels Rokat, and a passion to create only the best for businesses, large or small, ensures that every project will be fresh, unique and tailored to your needs or corporate image.
Rokat creates corporate identities, promotional material, book covers, packaging, posters, websites and any design project imaginable. Let your business blast off with Rokat.

RPBrown

Studio 11, 156 Parramatta Road
Camperdown NSW 2050

Phone: 02 9557 9078
Fax: 02 9557 9079
www.rpbrown.com
mrbrown@rpbrown.com

.........................p74

RPBrown produces ideas that turn heads. Mr Brown's approach to advertising and design is a seamless blend of concept and visual, to produce memorable communication and brand consistency across all mediums.

sam i am photo

Silver Pixel Studios
1/39 Phillip Street
Newtown NSW 2042

Phone: 02 9557 2550
Fax: 02 9557 2559
www.samiam.com.au
sam@samiam.com.au

........................p114

sam i am photo pride themselves on their artists. Producing a seamless job from concept to delivery is their aim. Representing a small group of artists whose work covers everything from fashion to food, cars to concords, sam i am photo has strengths in each area. A full service production company who enjoy translating the cerebral to the image… realising people's notions.
'Sam i am photo are an inspiring team to work with, resulting in a smooth sailing production on time and on budget.'
—Marcella Sullivan, HOST
'The photography was brilliant, the production superb and my tea had just the right amount of milk in it.'
—Paul Bruce, The Glue Society

Show & Tell Creative

Level 5, Studio 10
365 Little Collins Street
Melbourne VIC 3000

Phone: 03 8676 0366
Fax: 03 9670 2508
www.showandtell.com.au
studio@showandtell.com.au

........................p76

Located in the heart of Melbourne's CBD, Show & Tell is a dynamic design group providing creative outcomes in the areas of:
- Corporate identity development
- Stationery and marketing collateral
- Websites and content management
- Exhibition and display design

Our strategic approach ensures we deliver brilliant solutions for our clients where all areas of marketing and design reflect the style unique to each client's business. See what we have for show and tell today.

Simon Bowden Design (SB+D)

Level 1, 176 Burgundy Street
Heidelberg VIC 3084

Phone: 03 9458 2844
Fax: 03 9458 3877
www.sbdesign.net.au
info@sbdesign.net.au

........................p75

Simon Bowden Design drives to create a dynamic and striking concept for all our clients, while keeping their objective at the forefront of the design process.

Sprout Creative

Tiki Building
55 Hudson Fysh Avenue
Parap NT 0820

Phone: 08 8980 5700
Fax: 08 8980 5701
www.sprout.com.au
info@sprout.com.au

........................p78

Sprout Creative specialises in professional graphic design, multimedia, displays and websites. With a young and energetic design team based in Darwin, Sprout develops highly effective communication material from concept to campaigns and across-the-board media applications. Sprout prides itself on its originality and its understanding of context and environment. Sprout Creative's client base includes private and public organisations, and it is widely recognised as a leader of the creative industry in the Northern Territory.

Squidinc Illustration and Design

PO Box 456
Elwood VIC 3184

Phone: 03 9510 4552
Fax: 03 9525 1960
www.squidinc.com.au
shaun@squidinc.com.au

........................p106

Shaun Britton has worked as a designer and illustrator for Walt Disney and Warner Bros. Consumer Products for a number of years—in Hong Kong and in Australia. Since starting Squidinc, Shaun has worked with many clients, including Twentieth Century Fox, Nike, Coca Cola and Hallmark. His work is a blend of digital and traditional illustration and animation, playful graphic design and quirky character development.

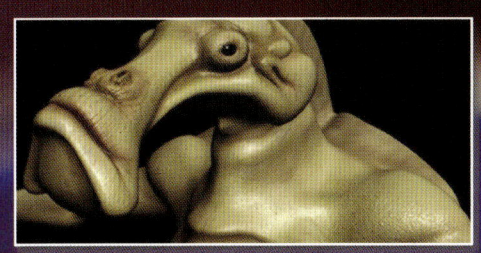

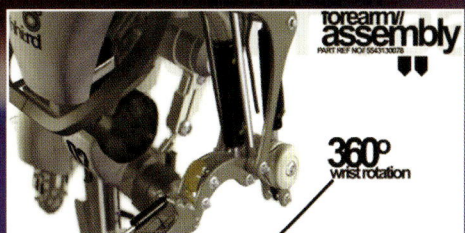

Start your exciting, creative career in digital media today!

3D Animation • Digital Film
Multimedia & Web Design • Graphic Design

Learn from professionals with real experience - Government accredited & AUSTUDY approved

Specialise in either 3D Max or Maya and learn how to create 3D animations and special effects for the film, gaming, architectural industries and more. Become an expert in storyboarding, modelling, texturing, lighting, photorealism, character design, rigging & animation, camera tracking, compositing, chroma-keying & scripting.

Study Graphic Design Production for pre-press and desktop publishing. All aspects of image capturing, generation, manipulation, correction and packaging for print are included in this course.

Online informaiton delivery will continue to grow in our computer oriented society. Learn multimedia design, programming, integration and production for the web, cd-rom and dvd delivery. Our course has evolved over the past 10 years from the web's infancy to the sophisticated means of delivery we have today.

Step into the rapidly evolving world of digital film, learn directing, camera work, scriptwriting and digital edting. Create documentaries, short films and music videos, in well-equipped and managed studios.

Studio218

PO Box 2143
Dickson ACT 2606

Phone: 02 6247 0059
Fax: 02 6249 7373
www.studio218.com.au
info@studio218.com.au

.........................p82

Studio218 is a Canberra based design studio. It successfully supplies fresh and innovative solutions to clients design and communication needs. Formerly known as Green Words & Images, Studio218 has wide experience in both private and public sectors and all areas of digital and print media. Studio218 specialises in publications, branding, corporate identity and websites from concept development to final design.

Storm Creative

Level 4, 8 West Street
North Sydney NSW 2060

Phone: 02 9922 1011
Fax: 02 9922 1444
www.stormcreative.com.au
mail@stormcreative.com.au

.........................p83

Storm Creative is a tenacious Sydney based creative agency riding a new wave. They have a passion for design, and focus on delivering top-notch creative, multimedia and web design. The Storm Creative philosophy is to do away with heavy advertising agency style infrastructure, keep business simple and employ highly creative experienced designers. This mix has seen Storm Creative experience continued success since its inception in 2000. When dealing with Storm Creative, clients deal directly with one designer from concept to completion, ensuring that designs are carried through efficiently (without the Chinese Whispers phenomenon) and the final product is reproduced to the standards that the designer intended. Brainstorming, regular creative meetings and office sports are all essential ingredients.

Studio Equator

Level 1, 225 Chapel Street
Prahran VIC 3181

Phone: 03 9510 8855
Fax: 03 9510 0188
www.studioequator.com
design@studioequator.com

.........................p80

Studio Equator harbours a collective group of young forward thinking designers who thrive on challenges. Offering a fresh approach and energetic level of experimentation, we act as an extension to our clients' business, cultivating their objectives together with our experiences, resulting in powerful communication and branding messages. Diversity and growth is our objective, design is our speciality.
We provide integrated disciplines within:
• Graphic Design—corporate identity & branding, environmental graphics & signage, publication, packaging, print, advertising design, web design,
• Interior Design—hospitality, fashion, retail, specialty shops and franchises.

Susy Boyer

PO Box 35
Miami QLD 4220

Phone: 07 5554 5394
Mobile: 0413 134 426
www.susyboyer.com
boyerart@bigpond.net.au

.........................p107

Susy Boyer has enjoyed life as a freelance illustrator for 19 years. She worked in Brisbane, Sydney and London before settling in her sunny beachside studio on the Gold Coast. A versatile artist, Susy illustrates mainly in hand-rendered watercolour, pencil and pastel, as well as fine art painting in pastel and acrylic on canvas. She works mainly in magazines, children's books and advertising. Her client list includes: World Vision, The Australian Women's Weekly, House & Garden, Slimming, Mother & Baby, Australian Parents, Penguin Books, Pearson Education, Scholastic, Macmillan, and Nelson.

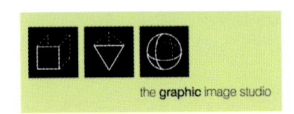

The Graphic Image Studio

6 Bastow Place
Mulgrave VIC 3170

Phone: 03 9562 1920
Fax: 03 9562 2585
www.tgis.com.au
studio@tgis.com.au

.........................p84

The Graphic Image Studio is an internationally recognised, award winning design studio specialising in architectural/interior design publications, corporate identity and packaging design. Established in 1989 and based in Melbourne, the team shares the vision of strong communication in print, producing high quality brochures, point-of-sale material and reports. Displaying a unique talent for theatrical promotion, the studio's work has featured in Hong Kong, Singapore, South Africa and the UK, as significant events tour the world.

The Targeted Approach to Recruitment

You know how crucial it is to secure the right permanent or freelance people - your business depends on it. When you contact Sage you are tapping into nearly 10 years of interviewing, testing, assessing and checking creative talent carried out by industry-experienced recruiters. As specialists in the creative industry, we can provide designers, operators, account service and support staff with the talent and the specialist skills to meet your brief.

Print or web we invest the time to ensure you get the right person, and we're so sure that we'll back them up with a unique guarantee of suitability. Plus a fixed fee, price competitive rate schedule and consultants that talk your language. Call us with your specific requirements. With over 5,000 quality candidates to choose from in our database you set the rules. Send us your detailed brief and we'll hit the bullseye with the best talent and skills available.

on target recruiting from

Sage
CREATIVE PLACEMENTS

Phone 9929 7486 Fax 9929 5171 email info@sagerecruit.com.au

Tracey Allen p85

PO Box 71
Ellendale TAS 7140

Mobile: 0408 207 270
www.traceyallen.com
tcallen@bigpond.com

Tracey Allen is a graphic designer, photographer and educator. For the past six years she has lectured at the University of Tasmania and the University of Technology, Sydney. Tracey established the student design studio at the University of Tasmania and has received several design awards. Tracey remains committed to her own design practice that includes corporate identity, publication and book design.

Triple 888 Studios p86

81-83 Wigram Street
Parramatta NSW 2150

Phone: 02 9891 2888
Fax: 02 9891 1283
www.triple888.com.au
designit@triple888.com.au

Triple 888 Studios provide creative artwork services of the highest standards with meticulous attention to detail, showcasing each client's products in the best way possible and creating long lasting partnerships.
Established in 1986, the studio has grown to provide creative design and strategic marketing services. Our strong design team has produced many award winning solutions—from packaging, brochures, corporate images, websites and advertisements. As a successful business, our services are employed by local and international clientele operating in a wide range of industries, including pharmaceutical, automotive, homewares, industrial, cosmetics and consumables.

Underline: Fitch p88

Level 11, 35 Clarence Street
Sydney NSW 2000

Phone: 02 9778 7474
Fax: 02 9778 7555
www.underline-fitch.com
info@underline-fitch.com

A multi discipline design consultancy providing Industrial, Interior and Graphic design through a network of studios in the Asia Pacific Region—Sydney, Singapore, Kuala Lumpur, Ho Chi Minh and Hong Kong through to China—Underline: Fitch provides a strategic approach to taking brands into the 'third dimension' of the retail environment. From the simplest expression of brand through packaging form and graphics to merchandising and creating the total retail environment, Underline: Fitch operates as the Asia Pacific arm of Fitch Global Studios. This ensures our designs reflect global trends while delivering innovative solutions to lead the local market.
Underline:Fitch believes it is vital to deliver the brand essence through the consistent application of the brand language at every consumer touch point. Based on this belief we have developed our consultancy over 25 years of operation to ensure our design and production capability can deliver on this principal. The ability of Underline: Fitch to work across a diverse and challenging range of projects, covering a broad geographic area, through our Asia Pacific network locally and the Fitch network globally, makes our consultancy the ideal choice for corporate identity or retail implementation programs. Underline: Fitch is skilled in concept presentation through our ability to present high definition virtual reality 3D modelling of product, packaging or environment. This style of presentation is available in either static or animated form as a virtual work around or walk through.

Visible Ink Design p87

Suite 5A, 4-6 Duke Street
Windsor VIC 3181

Phone: 03 9510 7455
Fax: 03 9510 4866
www.visibleink.com.au
visibleink@bigpond.com

Established in 1986, Visible Ink Design is a unique, award winning design studio highly regarded for its originality and quick response. From initial discussion through concept and design development, the studio prides itself on its close liaison with its clients at every stage of the process. Visible Ink's creative designs ensure an end product that goes beyond our client's expectations. Visible Ink specialises mainly in entertainment graphics, having packaged over 40 stage productions over the past six years. We're a design company small enough to respond quickly to a client's needs, but also large enough with the in-house facilities to manage the most comprehensive projects.

BEN RAPELL

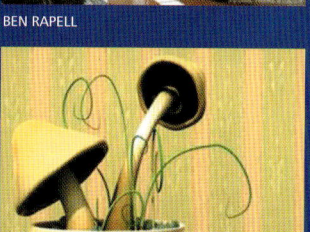

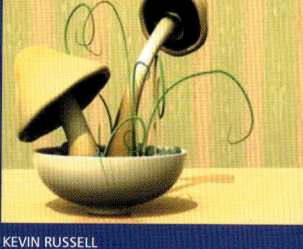

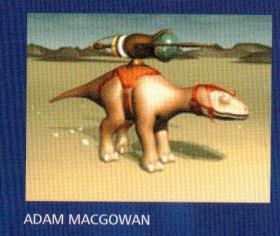

ADAM MACGOWAN

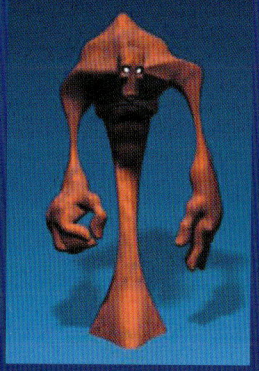

CRAIG DOYLE

KEVIN RUSSELL

TIM DAWSON

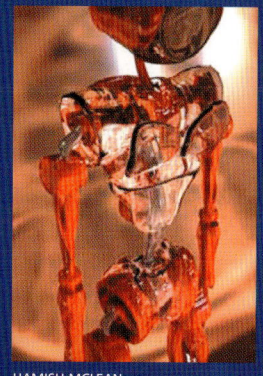

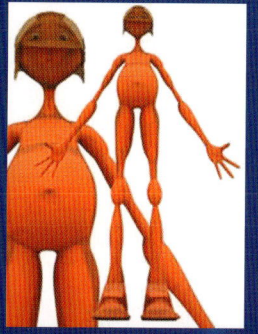

NEAL HARVEY

BRETT WHEELER

DAVID MCKENZIE

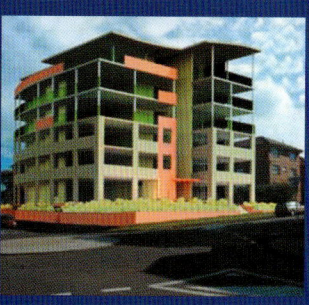

DAVID BROWN

CRAIG DOYLE

HAMISH MCLEAN

GLENN CHRISTENSEN

SIMON KRAMBOUSANOS

KEVIN RUSSELL

ADAM MACGOWAN

training for digital artists

Stunning digital content - award-winning animations - globally qualified artists. The results of **mad academy***'s 3d animation training speak for themselves. **mad academy*** graduates work in creative environments all over the world in the world's leading game, TV, film, and advertising production houses.

mad academy* inspires both newcomers and animation industry professionals to acquire knowledge of digital creation and production concepts that are relevant and sought after by film, television, architecture and games industries.

Short Courses
Whether you are an advanced user and work in the industry or a beginner and want to learn the basics of 3d Animation & Visual FX\Compositing software the **mad academy*** has a class designed especially for you. Classes offered are short, intensive and are geared towards giving you the best training possible.

TRAINING CENTER

discreet

Production companies prefer **mad academy*** students **mad academy*** students are getting employed! We are now constantly bombarded by production companies all over Australia looking to hire talent. The year 2004\2005 has found **mad academy*** students find work at some of Australia's leading production companies, a few examples are: Ambience, Inspiregen, Satchii & Satchii, Ivolve Studios, CG-Character, Plastic Wax, SthGraphics, True Life Creations, Monkey Lab, Ratbag.

3D Character Animator\Artist Course
Due to demand fueled by the quality of our shorter courses and the need for quality training and value both in time and price, we have created our 3D Character Animator\Artist Course. The aim of this 3.5 month full time intensive course is to prepare you for a career as a Professional 3D Artist.

Customised training
The **mad academy*** has extensive experience providing custom training for production studios, animation houses, corporations and individuals. We tailor our digital classes to fit your needs or create a class specifically for your artists.

Information evenings
The **mad academy*** holds free information evenings regularly at our training centres.

To book for one of these evenings or to receive a free program guide please call us on **1300 555 345** or visit our website

"Thank you, it was truly a motivating learning experience"

SHAN JOSEPH

mad academy*

www.madacademy.com.au

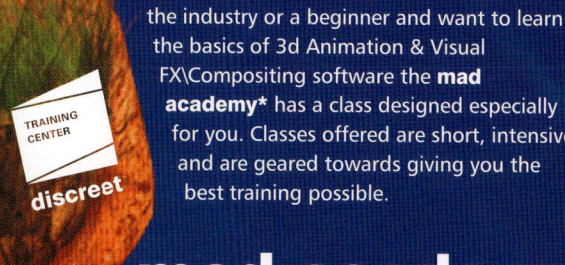

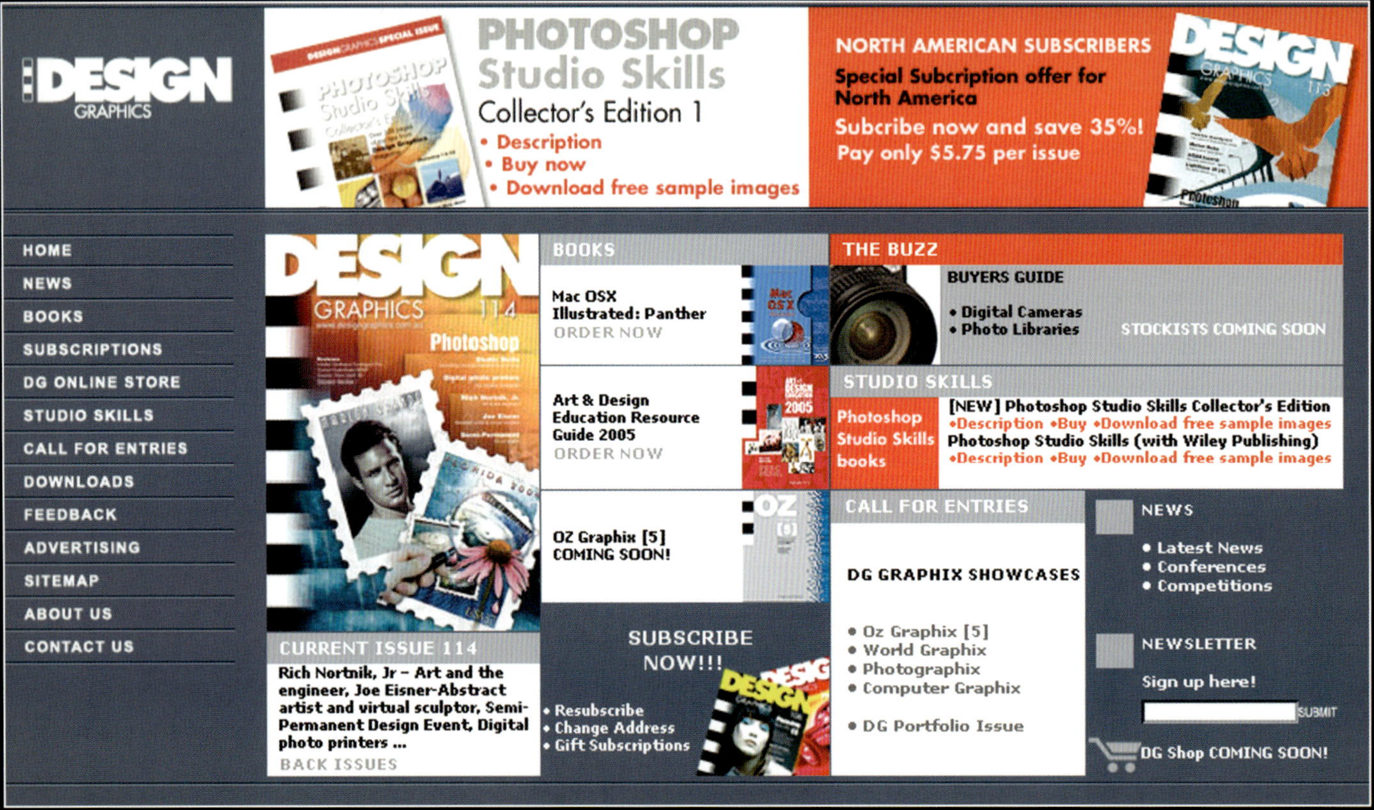

SUBSCRIBE NOW

Your complete guide to
digital publishing

www.designgraphics.com.au

DESIGN GRAPHICS SUBSCRIPTION FORM

Yes! I would like to subscribe to Design Graphics starting with:

☐ Current issue or .... ☐ Please indicate starting issue number

		1 year 12 issues Institution/corporate	1 year 12 issues Individual/Studio	1 year 12 issues Academic*
Australia inc. GST	Aust $	☐ 102.40	☐ 92.40	☐ 55.00
USA	US $	☐ 89.00	☐ 79.00	☐ 56.04
Canada	CN $	☐ 129.00	☐ 118.70	☐ 81.90
New Zealand	NZ $	☐ 138.00	☐ 128.00	☐ 90.00
UK	£	☐ 63.20	☐ 53.20	☐ 39.60
UK/Europe	Euro	☐ 88.32	☐ 78.32	☐ 58.32
Asia/Rest of World	Aust $	☐ 142.00	☐ 132.00	☐ 98.40

*Student subscribers must send a photocopy of a CURRENT student ID card with order

Mr/Mrs/Ms ....

Title ....

Company/Institution ....

You can also subscribe on our website at:
www.designgraphics.com.au

Address ....

....

Payment	AUSTRALIA
Cheque or	**Design Graphics**
credit card	A.B.N. 17 110 598 046
	PO Box 10
	Ferny Creek VIC 3786
	Australia

City/Suburb/Postcode ....

Country ....

Payment	USA & CANADA
Credit card only	

Telephone ....

Facsimile ....

Subscribe or resubscribe online
www.designgraphics.com.au

☐ Visa ☐ Mastercard ☐ American Express ☐ Bankcard

Australian subscribers may use cheque made payable to **Design Graphics**.

Subscription hot line	03 9760 1212
Credit card	International:
	61 3 9760 1212

Total amount payable $ [   ]

Facsimile	03 9755 1155
Credit card	International:
	61 3 9755 1155

Credit card number ....

Expiry date ....

Name on credit card ....

Email
subs@designgraphics.com.au

Signature ....

Subscribe to
PCGRAPHICS REPORT

www.pcgraphicsreport.com

Format	Regular price	Discount if ordered with Design Graphics
Print & PDF mailed to US/Canada	☐ US $119	☐ US $83
Print & PDF mailed internationally	☐ US $139	☐ US $97
PDF online only	☐ US $89	☐ US $63